The

Ferret

An Owner's Guide To

A HAPPY HEALTHY PET

Howell Book House

Howell Book House
A Simon & Schuster Macmillan Company
1633 Broadway
New York, NY 10019

MACMILLAN is a registered trademark of Macmillan, Inc.

Library of Congress Cataloging-in-Publication Data
Shefferman, Mary.
The ferret : an owner's guide to a happy, healthy pet / Mary Shefferman.
p. cm.
Includes bibliographical references.
ISBN 0-87605-498-X

1. Ferrets as pets. I. Title.
SF459.F47S465 1996
636′.974447—dc20   96-9030
                        CIP

Manufactured in the United States of America
10 9 8 7 6 5 4 3 2 1

Series Director: Dominique DeVito
Series Assistant Directors: Ariel Cannon
Book Design: Michele Laseau
Cover Design: Iris Jeromnimon
Illustration: Casey Price
Photography:
   Front cover: Adult: Renee Stockdale, Kit: Eric Shefferman
   Back cover: Renee Stockdale
   Susan Morrow: 16
   Eric Shefferman: 6, 7, 13, 18, 22, 24 ,25, 26, 28, 35, 43, 38, 53, 66, 68, 69, 93, 96, 105, 106, 112, 118
   Michael Siino: 34, 76, 85, 109, 110-111
   Renee Stockdale: 5, 10, 11, 12, 14, 15, 17, 19, 20, 21, 23, 29, 30, 31, 32-33, 37, 39, 45, 46, 40, 42, 49, 59, 60, 61, 62, 63, 64, 67, 70, 75, 79, 81, 87, 88, 89, 90-91, 92, 95, 98, 100, 102, 103, 104, 107, 110, 111, 114, 115, 117, 119
   Judith Strom: 56
   Faith Uridel: 9, 50, 113
Production Team: Kathleen Caulfield, John Ley, Christina Van Camp, Victor Peterson, Teresa Sheehan and John Carroll

Contents

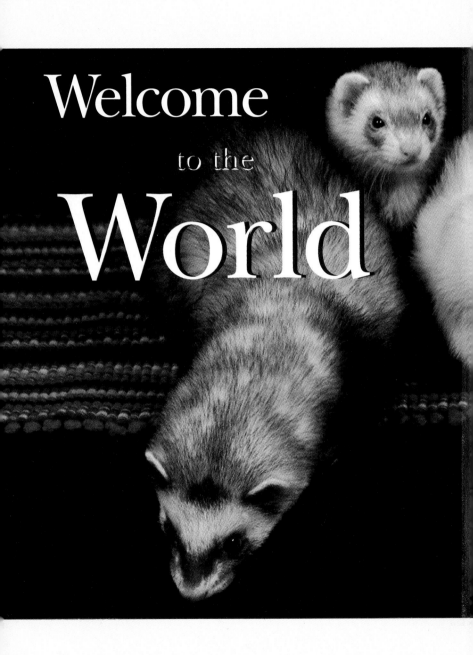

Welcome
to the
World

of the

Ferret

External Features of the Ferret

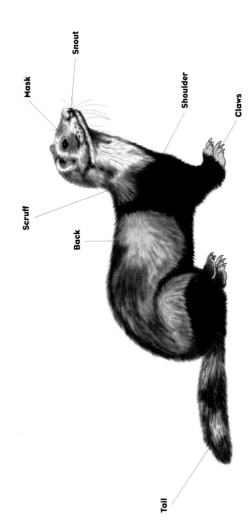

Snout

Mask

Shoulder

Claws

Scruff

Back

Tail

What
Is a
Ferret?

So what is a ferret? A ferret is a small, furry, carnivorous (meat-eating) mammal from the family *Mustelidae*. A ferret's scientific name is *Mustela furo*, although those who ascribe to the theory that the ferret is a domesticated version of a European polecat prefer *Mustela putorius furo*.

Many people mistakenly believe that the ferret is the wild North American Black-Footed Ferret or another kind of wild animal. In fact, the ferret is a domesticated animal, not a wild animal who has been tamed or raised in captivity. The ferret was domesticated several thousand years ago to help hunters flush rabbits from their warrens (holes) and pursue small pests like rats and mice. (See

Chapter 2, "History and Ancestry of the Ferret," for more information.)

In some European countries and Australia, the ferret still works at "ferreting out" rabbit warrens for hunters

Today, the ferret has earned the title of the third most popular companion mammal.

who set nets to catch the fleeing rabbits. But here in the United States, the ferret has retired from the working life and taken up the title of third most popular companion mammal. The ferret has earned a place of honor beside the dog and cat in the laps of hundreds of thousands of humans.

In this role, the ferret performs many equally important functions. The ferret is curiosity in a fur coat. He is playful, highly inquisitive, fearless and friendly. The ferret has a sense of humor. He is intelligent and resourceful. His shape is elegant and his energy is boundless. A ferret is exuberant, affectionate and athletic (though a bit less than graceful). Above all, the ferret is simply adorable.

The Basic Information

Male ferrets are called *hobs* and females are called *jills*. A castrated male is called a *gib* and a spayed female is called a *sprite*. Baby ferrets are called *kits*. Females can be a little more fidgety than males. As males get older, they are more likely to turn into lap ferrets than females—but there are really no absolutes.

Hobs and gibs are up to 50 percent larger than jills and sprites. Hobs are usually between three and five pounds at maturity, while jills are usually between one and a half and three pounds. Ferrets neutered when they are very young do not usually get as big as those neutered after they reach six months old. For example, all four of our ferrets were altered when they were very young and they range in weight from one and a half pounds to three pounds—females and males. But we know some whole (intact) male ferrets that are between five and seven pounds. Some jills can be as big as a gib who was neutered young.

Life Span

Ferrets live between six and ten years. We've heard of ferrets who lived to be twelve years old, but more commonly they live to seven or eight years. Ferrets are considered to be geriatric by the time they're four years old. Although genetics plays a large part in the longevity of ferrets, the care they receive plays a large role as well. Even the heartiest of ferrets will not do well if he is not fed proper food, kept in good health and given lots of love and affection.

> **FERRET LANGUAGE**
>
> Male ferrets are hobs and female ferrets are jills. A castrated male is a gib and a spayed female is a sprite. Names for groups of animals often come from observations about the behavior of those animals. It is not surprising, then, that a group of ferrets is called a *business*.

These ferret kits have the elegance, curiosity and just plain cuteness that make the ferret an attractive pet.

Vocalization

Ferrets are quiet animals, for the most part. Many will make a kind of chittering-type noise that sounds like "dook, dook, dook" when they are excited or playing. Sabrina is the only one of our ferrets who makes this noise regularly, and she does it only in response to the sound of a squeak toy.

A ferret will hiss as a sort of warning to another ferret who's annoying him. When ferrets play together (and they can play rough), they tend to make a good deal of noise. Sometimes it sounds like they're hurting each other, but when you separate the two ferrets they go right back to play fighting. If a ferret is hurt, there is no mistaking the shriek.

Meat Eaters

Ferrets are carnivores, which means their teeth are designed for tearing and eating meat. Their canine teeth are long and, in most ferrets, stick out beyond the lips.

Ferret Odor

All mustelids have a characteristic musky aroma. The ferret has scent glands all over his body, including an anal scent glad that he can "express" in much the same way the skunk does, as a form of protection. However, the odor from a ferret's anal scent gland is not as pungent or as lingering as the odor from a skunk. Except in rare cases, a ferret will not express his anal scent gland unless he is frightened or feels threatened. For the most part, it is impossible to tell whether or not a ferret has been descented unless he has recently expressed the scent gland.

Ferrets in heat (jills) or rut (hobs) do smell, but because it is highly recommended that pet ferrets be neutered (females can die from complications of prolonged heat), you will not have to worry about that odor.

> **THE FERRET'S RELATIVES**
>
> The ferret's closest relatives are the polecat, weasel and mink. Other relatives are the ermine (winter coat) or stoat (summer coat), skunk, otter, wolverine and the endangered North American Black-Footed Ferret (BFF). The ferret is the only domesticated member of the family.

COLORS AND MARKINGS

You should choose your ferret based on his personality, but seasoned ferret owners know that "I don't have that color" is a good excuse to get another ferret.

Considering that ferrets are little thieves, one of the most appropriate markings on a ferret is the mask. Masks can be a band across the eyes or shaped like a V. Some are clearly delineated and others sort of trail off into the other color on the ferret's face. Often the guard hairs, the longer hairs in the coat, are a different color from the undercoat, which is the softer, shorter fur. Ferrets' coat colors often change slightly from season to season, and sometimes the shape of the mask will change slightly as well.

FERRET COLORS

Ferrets come in many different colors. Sable (dark brown) and chocolate (light brown) are the most common. Another common color (actually lack of color) is albino. Albino ferrets are white with red eyes. Other colors include champagne (cream-colored), cinnamon (reddish) and silver (light gray).

Ferrets come in many different colors and have different markings. Pictured here are an albino and three sables.

Ferrets come in various colors, sable (dark brown) or chocolate (light brown) being the most common. Other colors include: champagne or butterscotch (cream or pale brown), cinnamon (reddish), silver (grayish), black- or dark-eyed white (a rare coloring) and albino, sometimes called "red-eyed white." Albino ferrets are relatively common. Some ferret enthusiasts theorize that the albino is the "purest" form of the ferret, while others believe the sable coloring to be the pure form.

Ferrets also often have markings or patterns. One of the most common patterns is the Siamese or color point pattern, where the legs, tail and mask (referred to as "points") are considerably darker than the body, and the mask is shaped like a V. Another common pattern is the solid or self pattern, where the body and points are the same color. Additionally, there's the standard pattern, in which the points are only a little darker than the body.

The panda ferret pattern is characterized by a white head, bib and feet. There is no mask on a panda. Blaze (also called badger or shetland) is a marking type that is characterized by a white stripe on the top of the head, with white fur at the knees and feet or toe tips. Blazes have white bibs and often have dark smudgelike markings around their eyes instead of a mask. When a ferret is called a silver mitt, it means he is that color and has four white feet—mitts are simply white feet.

Ferrets need training, socializing and loving attention—the more the better!

Some consider the panda and blaze markings to be a sign of Waardensburg syndrome, in which white fur on the head is genetically linked to deafness. Our Ralph is a blaze and he is deaf. However, ferrets get most of their information from their sense of smell, and deafness doesn't seem to be a problem for Ralph at all. Some deaf ferrets might be more easily upset by sudden movements than hearing ferrets. The link between deafness and the white markings is apparently not an absolute, as some breeders have said that they have bred blaze-marked ferrets that are not deaf.

Albinos are not more prone to blindness. Albinism is actually a fairly common feature in ferrets, and is desirable. (I know we love ours!)

Before you decide to get a ferret, be sure you are willing to make the necessary adjustments to your home to keep this little explorer safe.

Is the Ferret the Right Pet for You?

After addressing the basics, it is now time to ask yourself if the ferret is indeed the right pet for you. It is important to be sure a ferret is right for you before you bring one home.

DO YOU MIND THE SMELL?

As we mentioned above, ferrets have a special smell. In fact, all animals have their own particular odor, and ferrets are no exception. It isn't that ferrets smell more than other animals, but that they smell different from what most people are used to. Some people do not like the ferret's musky aroma. Others think it's earthy and pleasant.

DO YOU HAVE THE TIME AND ATTENTION TO GIVE?

You cannot get a ferret and leave it in its cage all the time. They must get exercise every day for several (two or more) hours. Ferrets are very social and need companionship. If you will not be able to spend a lot of time playing with your ferret (which means getting on the floor and *playing*), you should consider getting two ferrets, or none at all.

Ferrets will entertain you with their hilarious antics and eager personalities.

CAN YOU MAKE THE NECESSARY ADJUSTMENTS TO YOUR HOME?

Ferrets like to burrow. They like to hide and sleep in dark places, under blankets and in clothes baskets. Some ferrets are diggers. If you are not willing to make some adjustments for ferret behaviors, a ferret might not be the best pet for you. For example, some ferrets dig at carpeting or in plants. Are you willing to put a plastic runner on your carpet and move your plants out of your ferret's reach? Ferrets are very curious and persistent—they like to interact with things to see what will happen. No open beverage or delicate object is 100 percent safe from an exploring ferret. Ferret-proofing is never done; are you willing to make adjustments to your ferret's environment to keep him safe?

Ferrets are loving, affectionate, funny, entertaining animals who are willing to adapt to your lifestyle. Are you willing to meet them halfway? They'll rearrange

FERRET FACTS

- There are an estimated 5 to 7 million pet ferrets in the US today.

- A ferret's life expectancy is 6 to 10 years.

- Ferrets were probably domesticated by Europeans who used them for hunting rabbits. The first ferrets came to the United States over 300 years ago on ships in which they were used for rodent control.

their sleeping hours (all sixteen-plus of them) so they can play when you're available. Will you take the time to play with them? Are you willing to have litter boxes in each room your ferret will have access to?

Can You Afford the Expense?

Ferrets need a good ferret food or high-quality kitten food, which can be a bit expensive. Can you afford that expense? Can you afford the yearly vaccinations and potentially serious illnesses your ferret might get when he is older? Some ferret behaviors can be exasperating. Do you have the patience to look after a perpetually inquisitive animal?

Ferrets are wonderful pets for the right people. After having dogs, cats, guinea pigs, gerbils and mice, I can say that I've never had a pet as lovable, entertaining or affectionate as a ferret.

History
and Ancestry
of the Ferret

Not very much is known about the history of the ferret. There are stories and myths, but not very much hard evidence about where these little animals come from or when, exactly, they were domesticated. The only sure thing is that an animal fitting the description of a ferret appears in some ancient writings.

The Ferret's Ancient Origins

So when was the ferret domesticated, and by whom? Some say the Egyptians domesticated the ferret a few hundred years before they domesticated the cat. This is based on an Egyptian hieroglyphic depicting an animal that looks like a ferret. Some argue that the animal could be a mongoose, which has a shape similar to a ferret's and which was commonly used in Egypt to keep homes free of snakes and other pests. It is also argued that because ferrets are particularly susceptible to extreme heat, which is common in North Africa, it is unlikely that the animal in the hieroglyphic is a ferret at all.

This ferret is posing with tamer versions of his relatives, the otter and the skunk.

It isn't until Aristophanes's time (450–425 B.C.) that there are written accounts of an animal that fits the description of a ferret or a domesticated polecat. In 350 B.C., Aristotle used the same word Aristophanes had used to describe an animal that was probably a truly domesticated ferret. Just because there wasn't a separate word to differentiate the ferret from its wilder ancestors doesn't mean there wasn't a difference. Language often takes some time to catch up with evolution. Even today some European languages use the same word to describe ferrets and polecats, though the two are different animals.

FERRETING

In ancient Greece and medieval England (among other places) ferrets hunted with humans, helping to flush rabbits out of their dens. Ferreting is illegal in the United States, but is still practiced in England. Ferret racing, also practiced in the United Kingdom, is a related activity in which the ferrets race through plastic and mesh tunnels designed to simulate the earthen tunnels of their natural working environment.

By Roman times, the ferret was most certainly domesticated. The use of ferrets in flushing rabbits from their holes (called "ferreting") was widespread by this

time. By the end of the Roman Empire, ferreting
was common throughout Europe, primarily practiced
by peasants.

Working Heritage

Ferrets have done their share of work. They will not
only chase rabbits from their warrens, but they are also
excellent mousers and ratters. In ancient times, the
Phoenicians likely used ferrets on their ships to keep
them free of rats and mice. They were used throughout Europe for centuries to control rodent problems
in homes and barns. During the Revolutionary War,
ferrets were used on American ships to control
rodents. Ferrets have also been used to run wire
through narrow tubing in aircraft.

*The European
polecat,* Mus-
tela putorius, *is widely considered the clos-
est ancestor of
the ferret. This
one was raised
in captivity.*

The Ferret's Ancestors

Figuring out how the ferret evolved is not as simple as
you might think. Usually archaeological evidence
helps scientists piece together the route of evolution of
domesticated animals from their wild ancestors.
Because many of the physical characteristics (that is,
bones, skulls, etc.) of the ferret's closest relatives are
hard to distinguish from others in the family, it is
nearly impossible to determine where one species ends
and the other begins.

The ferret's scientific name is either *Mustela furo* or
Mustela putorius furo, depending on which theory you

follow. In either case, the word *furo* means thief, an appropriate title for an animal who steals and hides the things it treasures. *Furo* is from the same Latin root as the word *furtive,* which shows that the ferret was aptly named.

The word ferret, derived from the Latin word for thief, is an appropriate name for this little criminal.

It is a widely held belief that the closest ancestor of the ferret is *Mustela putorius,* the European polecat. Those that ascribe to this theory refer to the ferret as *Mustela putorius furo,* meaning that the ferret is a subspecies of the European polecat. The theory is supported by the similarities between the two animals, including their having the same number of chromosomes and similar colorings. The fact that they can breed with each other and produce fertile offspring further supports this theory. It is important to remember, however, that these two are not the same species, despite their similarities.

FAMOUS OWNERS OF FERRETS

Queen Elizabeth I

Donna Rice

Dick Smothers

Dave Foley

Another theory once widely held is that the ferret is a domesticated form of the steppe polecat *(Mustela eversmanni).* More accurate testing has since shown this possibility is less likely than the European polecat theory.

Although it may be impossible to know for certain what the truth is regarding the ferret's ancestry, it is certain that the ferret is most closely related to some type of polecat.

Famous Ferrets

Ferrets have appeared in various paintings throughout history. There is a portrait of Queen Elizabeth I with one of her albino ferrets. Ferrets also appear in paintings by Domenico di Bartolo (*Pope Celestinus III Grants Privilege of Independence to the Spedale*) and Leonardo da Vinci (*Lady with Ermine*).

In Europe, ferrets were used by peasants to flush rabbits out of their holes. In the United States today, they are hardworking pets.

Not satisfied with a modeling career, the ferret has taken up acting. Ferrets have had roles in movies such as *Kindergarten Cop* with Arnold Schwarzenegger, the *Beastmaster* movies with Marc Singer and a brief part in *Legends of the Fall*. They're not always portrayed accurately, as evidenced by the unferret-like sounds they make in *Beastmaster*. But they do sometimes get an image boost. In *Kindergarten Cop* one of the children asks if Arnold's ferret bites. Arnold replies very seriously, "He never bites." This long-awaited and well-deserved good publicity for ferrets was greatly appreciated by ferret lovers everywhere.

The ferret has also had small roles on some television shows, such as *Northern Exposure* and *Second Noah*. There's even a Muppet that looks very much like a ferret (though it may actually be a weasel). On television, ferrets are probably referred to more often than seen. David Letterman has mentioned ferrets several times in his "Top Ten" list. Ferrets also got a mention once on the series *Mad About You.* The lack of ferrets on the small and large screens is most likely due to the difficulty in keeping ferrets focused long enough to shoot a scene. Dogs do much better than ferrets when it comes to following commands. The fact that ferrets are illegal in California (even in Hollywood) is probably another reason we don't see more famous ferrets in movies and on television.

Ferrets are certainly photogenic, but they have a hard time keeping still long enough for film performances.

Queen Elizabeth I was not the only famous person to own ferrets. Some other famous ferret owners past and present include James Doohan and his wife Wende, Donna Rice, Dick Smothers and Dave Foley.

3

The **World** According to the **Ferret**

If ferrets could talk, they'd most likely say things like "Everything on the floor is mine!" "What's this?" and "Look at *me*!" Ferrets are hypercurious bundles of energy when they are young, and retain this energy level throughout most of their lives. They balance this intense energy with deep, relaxed sleep. They are extremely social and enjoy interacting with people and other animals. Ferrets have their own personalities, and each will have his own favorite toys, games, treats, hiding places and sleeping spots. They are very intelligent and will quickly learn what they can get away with. They will even try to train you to do what they want. Every ferret is unique and it is important to realize that there are no hard and fast rules.

Ferrets Need Training and Supervision

A ferret's personality is as much a product of his upbringing as a dog's personality is a product of *his* upbringing. How you train, socialize and treat your ferret will go further in determining his personality than anything else. The more love and affection you show your ferret, the more he will show toward you and the friendlier he will be toward others. Ferrets are smart animals who will learn the limits you set, but if you don't set limits they will make up their own. A ferret given no guidance is like a dog or a child given no guidance—a creature you'd prefer to avoid. Given love and a set of reasonable rules, a ferret makes a warm and wonderful pet.

Ferrets will get into anything if given half a chance, so they need to be supervised closely.

You will be hard-pressed to find a ferret owner who does not refer to his ferrets as children, babies, kids or little ones. Because they require a close eye, they are very much like toddlers—getting into everything. Ferrets are dependent on us, their owners, for everything from food and shelter to love and attention. They are truly domesticated animals who need human intervention in order to survive. Scientists describe the behaviors of the ferret species as juvenile, which is common in domesticated species. They no longer have the instincts to take care of themselves outside a human environment.

21

Ferrets Love Company

Ferrets are very social animals. They enjoy the company of other ferrets and humans. Because ferrets have little sense of personal space, they are usually not possessive of food and will all eat from the same bowl. All our ferrets share the same food dish, water bottles, hammocks and litter boxes. There's no fighting over the food, though there is occasionally a line at the litter box. Although they are not territorial, you will notice one of the bunch emerging as the boss, or alpha, ferret. You'll notice that when another ferret joins the group, the alpha ferret will be the one the new one wrestles with most at first.

If You Have More Than One Ferret

When ferrets are young, their mothers teach them how to behave with one another. Littermates wrestle and play together, testing each other's tolerance levels for biting and playing. As we said above, ferrets are very social animals, so it might seem unusual that some ferrets don't like other ferrets. But it can happen. Ferrets

Ferrets usually get along well and will be wonderful playmates for each other.

are individuals and will like or dislike some other ferrets just as you or I might dislike a particular person. Whole (not neutered) males can be downright dangerous to other male ferrets when they are in season.

If your ferret has been an only ferret for a year or more, he might feel threatened by other ferrets. Some ferrets scream in fear when another ferret tries to initiate play. Whenever you have a situation in which one ferret is frightened of another or the two ferrets dislike each other, you must proceed with caution. Ferrets can hurt each other very badly (even kill each other) when they mean to do so. How do you know if you have a problem?

Supervise any new introductions very closely. Although ferrets play very roughly with each other, sometimes it is more than play. If either ferret draws blood from the other, separate them immediately. If you're introducing a kit into an adult group, the kit will probably get dragged around a bit. When we brought home Knuks, the other ferrets took turns trying to drag her off to their secret hiding places. They weren't trying to hurt Knuks, but they did annoy her—they kept interfering with her exploration of her new environment. It's usually a good idea to keep the new ferret in a separate cage until you are sure everyone gets along. For kits, it gives them some time to get a little bigger and more confident before they're locked into a cage with a bunch of big, sometimes bullying, ferrets.

Ferret behavior is different from that of dogs and cats. Who would guess that this is an expression of excitement?

Following are some strategies to bring ferrets together. You can switch the bedding of the two ferrets so they can get used to each other's smell. This often works for ferrets who aren't trying to kill each other. Another option is to put the two cages next to each other, so the two ferrets can see each other, but not hurt each other. Bathing both ferrets in a perfumed shampoo can help reduce animosity between them. Remember that ferrets get much of their information from their sense of smell; in many cases the ferrets don't like or are not used to the smell of each other. Some acceptance problems may take months to resolve; others may never be.

Normal Ferret Behavior

Ferret body language is different from the body language of dogs and cats. The unfamiliarity of the ferret's body language can sometimes confuse or frighten the uninitiated.

STEALING AND HIDING STUFF

The word *ferret* is from the Latin root *fur,* the same root that gives us the word *furtive.* The animal is aptly named. One of the ferret's favorite activities is stealing and hiding things. Different ferrets have different tastes. Almost all ferrets like to steal leather (key chains, gloves, shoes). Many like to steal socks (especially dirty ones). Some like to steal plastic or rubber things. Your ferret will have his own peculiar tastes.

Regardless of what your ferret likes to steal, he'll probably find an out-of-the-way place to hide it. Our Sabrina used to put my shoes behind the couch and had been seen once or twice dragging a rubber chicken across the living room (we now know that latex rubber chickens are a big no-no for ferrets). Ralph takes pens. Knuks likes to drag the cat carrier around (an amusing sight, indeed!). Marshmallow hides pieces of hard food in a canvas bag the ferrets sort of adopted as a sleeping spot. Most ferrets hide food "for later." It has nothing to do with how much you feed them. If your ferret tends to steal things you need regularly (like your keys), you should probably make a note of where he keeps them.

A toy dangling overhead can make an enthusiastic ferret leave the ground!

DANCE OF JOY

This is the dance of the ferret. The ferret will hop about, often backward or sideways, with reckless abandon and with its mouth wide open. Bouncing off walls and furniture is common. This can frighten people who don't understand ferret behavior, but it is actually just your ferret's way of expressing how happy he is and how much energy he has.

SLEEPING

Ferrets like to sleep, often sixteen to eighteen hours per day. If they are left alone in their cage with nothing to do, they will usually just go to sleep. This means that when you are ready to play with them, they will be fully recharged and ready to go. Ferrets' bodies can be especially limp when they are sleeping, so it is important to support them very carefully. Ferret kits sleep very deeply. One theory is that this deep sleep is a defense mechanism inherited from a wild ancestor. If a predator finds an apparently dead animal, it will not eat it. Thus, a baby ferret in a deathlike sleep would be safe. Sometimes ferrets who are sick or old will sleep deeply also.

Ferrets like to sleep cuddled together in a pile.

YAWNING

Ferrets yawn a lot. It's very cute, and can be contagious. It comes with the territory of sleeping a lot.

SHIVERING

Your ferret's body temperature drops while he's sleeping, and when he first awakens he may need to warm himself up. Likewise, if your hands are cold and you pick up your ferret, he will probably shiver. It's important to note that he is not afraid, just cold. Shivering is not a fear reaction; frightened ferrets usually stay very still.

LITTER BOX QUIRKS

Ferrets have a very quick metabolism and need to both eat and use the litter box throughout the day. Often they will need to "go" within a few minutes of waking up. Most ferrets are excellent when it comes to using the litter box in their cage. To help keep your ferret on his best behavior, wake him up a few minutes before you want to let him out of the cage for play time. You may be able to get him to use the box before he comes out to play and thus help prevent accidents outside the cage.

Ferrets can be fussy about exactly how and where they are standing in the litter box. They often hop in and out of the litter box several times, sniff at the litter box and position and reposition before they actually use the box.

Any ferret will tell you that the proper place to poop is in a corner. Because of their quick metabolism, when ferrets have to go, they *have* to go. They will search for the best available corner (a ferret's bathroom motto is: "any corner in an emergency!"). To ensure that your ferret uses the litter box, place litter boxes in all of his favorite corners. If for some reason you want to discourage the use of a particular corner, try placing a food bowl or a bedding towel there. Ferrets won't poop in their food or in a good place to sleep.

Ferrets sleep—and yawn—a lot.

After using the litter box, ferrets like to wipe their behinds on the ground, which often means on your carpeting. Although this can be a sign of parasites in a dog, it is normal behavior for a ferret. Some people put small replaceable "wiping rugs" near the favorite boxes.

Ferrets usually understand that they are supposed to use their litter box and that not using it upsets their owners. They will sometimes go in a place they know is inappropriate (even right next to the litter box) in order to protest anything from an insufficiently cleaned litter box to having a toy taken away from them to not getting enough attention.

Chewing on Bad Things

Ferrets use their mouths like people use their hands. Ferrets like to grab things, pull on things and chew on things. Some of these things they don't intend to eat, like rubber bands, ear plugs, sponges, paper, and so on, but if a piece accidentally breaks off, they may not be able to do anything but swallow it. These pieces can lodge in their stomach or intestines and cause a life-threatening blockage (see chapter 7).

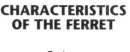

CHARACTERISTICS OF THE FERRET
Curious
Likes to burrow and hide
Extremely active
Playful
Friendly
Needs a totally "ferret-proof" environment
Requires training, attention and affection
Litter box training may not be 100 percent effective

It is important to note the types of dangerous things your ferret tries to chew on and keep them away from him. Marshmallow likes to chew on plastic bags, paper and rubber bands. He is usually caught in the act because you can hear him coughing and choking. After we pull a piece of paper out of his mouth that he was choking on, he will immediately try to grab and chew on the piece of paper again. There's something he likes about chewing on certain textures, and we have to be very careful what we leave in his reach.

Self-Cleaning

A ferret will sometimes try to get his smell "just right" by licking his front paws and using them to wipe from behind his ears down to his face. It looks like he is trying to wash his face. Actually, he is picking up ferret scent from the scent glands behind his ears and using it to improve his aroma.

Flat Ferret

When bored or while pondering what to do next, ferrets may lie down flat on their stomachs and just stay still. It may be time for you to play with them or find them another toy.

ITCHING

Ferrets are very itchy animals and they scratch an awful lot. They will sometimes even stop mid-run, scratch an itch and then keep running as if they never stopped. They sometimes wake up and suddenly have to scratch somewhere.

Ralph treats this plastic ball like a baby ferret. He gives it a chance to eat and sleep and becomes protective when another ferret gets interested in his special toy.

If your ferret scratches more than usual or if you notice fur missing or a rash, there may be a problem. Consider all the things that touch your ferret's skin: bedding, what the bedding is washed in, whether you use dryer sheets, and so forth. Try to eliminate the cause of the irritation. If the itching becomes severe or your ferret's skin becomes raw, seek advice from your veterinarian.

COMMON FERRET BEHAVIORS

To the uninitiated, these behaviors may seem strange. As you get to know your ferret, you will become familiar with these and many other unique activities.

Sleeping sixteen to eighteen hours a day

Yawning

Stealing and hiding objects

Shivering

Itching

Digging

FETISHES

Different ferrets can fall in love with different items. Our Ralph has a plastic ball he treats like a baby ferret. He protects it and occasionally carries it around to show it the surroundings. He sometimes even leaves it in the food bowl for a while to give it a chance to eat. When he is done with it, he places it back in its own special spot. If another ferret plays with it, he will grab it away and return it to its spot. He even went through a phase where he would scream whenever Marshmallow tried to take it away from him.

BOTTLEBRUSH TAIL

When a ferret is excited, the hair on his tail may stand on end, resembling a bottlebrush. This is sometimes a fear/anger reaction (as when fighting with another ferret), and sometimes a "what's this new stuff?" reaction (as when brought into new surroundings).

FERRET PLAY

It seems that ferrets live to play. But their play behavior can be mistaken for real fighting if you are unfamiliar with what they are doing. Below are some of the normal things ferrets do to amuse themselves.

Wrestling

Ferrets need to figure out who is boss. They will play fight with each other to find out. When a new ferret is introduced he will need to find out where he stands with each of the other ferrets. Often the larger, older ferret will grab the smaller, younger ferret by the scruff of the neck and drag him around. As we

discussed above, sometimes two ferrets will not get along, and you will have to take special measures to introduce them to each other. More often ferrets go through a brief adjustment period and sort things out on their own.

Ferrets are active animals who love to play with you or each other.

Exercise Time

Ferrets have a lot of energy and need to expend it by having some running-around time every day. They will get very frustrated and stressed if left in their cage for too long without a chance to run. If you want to spend some quality time holding and stroking your ferret, you will find him much more cooperative after he has had some exercise.

Moving Things Around

Ferrets like to move things around. They can drag some incredibly heavy objects, and have an incredible amount of determination. If a boot can't fit under the couch, they will keep on trying. Pushing a ball (we like to use hollow plastic Easter eggs) around on the floor with his nose is a fun game for the ferret, and funny to watch. Many ferrets will lie on top of small round objects and move them by scooting backward. This is another behavior the ferret inherited from his wild ancestors, who moved eggs in this manner. The ferret's wild behavior, however, is half gone as a result of domestication, and most ferrets have no clue what to do with the object once they've moved it across the floor.

Wrestling is a way for ferrets to play and determine who's boss.

Digging

The ferret's ancestors were burrowing animals, so ferrets like to dig at things or run their noses through them. Most ferret owners keep their plants well out of reach of their ferrets. The food bowl or litter box can be fun to "nosedive" through, and some ferrets will even try to nosedive through a bowl of water. If your ferret throws litter and food around, he might be trying to tell you he's upset about something (like you're not giving him enough attention). Ferrets consider tissue boxes to be a great find, because the more they keep digging at them, the more tissues keep coming out. Some ferret owners keep a kiddie pool filled with clean damp sand for their ferrets to burrow through.

To a ferret, a tissue box is a great place to dig.

Carpet Scratching

Some ferrets like to scratch at carpet. They can seem to sit and scratch endlessly at carpet, usually in a corner or in front of a closed door. Their great determination makes it unlikely that they will just give up. For a short-term solution, you can distract them with a toy. For a long-term solution, you may want to place a plastic carpet runner over the area to prevent your ferret from damaging the carpet, The plastic doesn't have the same alluring texture as the carpet, so your ferret is less likely to dig at it. Other options are tacking a carpet sample, which can be replaced periodically, over your carpet or removing the carpeting altogether.

Chasing

Along with mock combat and wrestling, chase is another favorite ferret game. Ferrets will often chase each other all around—if several ferrets are involved it can resemble a high-speed conga line. If you get down on the floor with your ferret you may find that he is interested in playing with you, too.

31

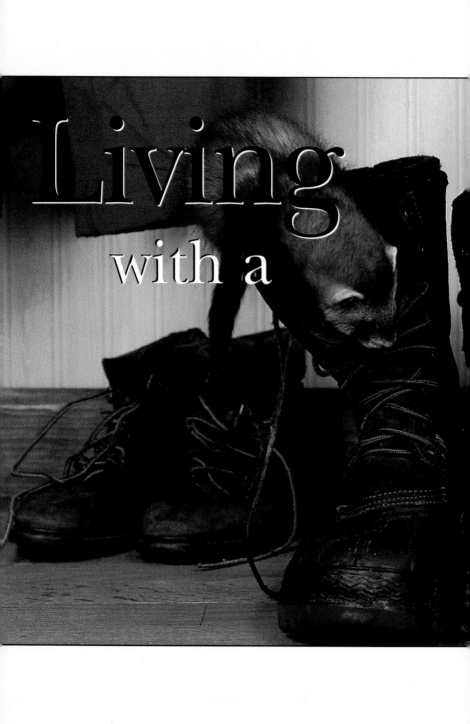

Living

with a

part two

Ferret

Bringing Your
Ferret
Home

Where to Buy Your Ferret

PET SHOPS

The majority of ferrets in the United States come from large breeder farms that supply the animals to pet shops. These farms routinely neuter and descent (remove the anal scent gland from) the baby ferrets before they even reach the pet shops. Many of the kits sold in pet shops have two small bluish tattoos on their ear flaps. These indicate that the ferret has been neutered and descented.

PRIVATE BREEDERS

There are also smaller, private breeders who sell kits directly to pet owners. Private breeders generally do not neuter the kits before they sell them, recommending instead that the new ferret owner wait until the ferret is at least six months old (fully mature) before having this surgery performed. Sex hormones play a significant role in helping the ferret mature. Waiting until the ferret has reached full maturity before neutering him gives him the opportunity to grow with the benefit of sex hormones. Ferrets who are neutered later in life not only may be larger than those that are neutered early on, they may be healthier as well.

The kit you purchase at a pet store will most likely be neutered and descented already.

FERRET SHELTERS

Ferrets are also available through a ferret shelter/rescue. Most animal shelters that take in cats and dogs do not take in or adopt out ferrets, but they might have information on how to find a ferret shelter near you. Most adoptees are wonderful animals whose original owners didn't do their research before bringing home a ferret. Few, if any, ferrets are beyond rehabilitation. They come around with love and attention. A reputable ferret shelter will not attempt to place a ferret inappropriately. You will most likely have to answer questions about your home and sign a contract in order to adopt a ferret. See chapter 13 for how to contact S.T.A.R.* Ferrets, a national network of ferret shelters, for a shelter in your area.

Choosing a Ferret

It is often recommended that new ferret owners get an adult ferret as their first ferret. This depends on what your household is like and how comfortable you feel with the training of a kit.

If you've had experience training a puppy, training a kit will come relatively easily. This may influence your decision regarding getting an adult versus a baby ferret. If you've never had an animal that requires socialization and training, you might want to look into getting an adult.

In choosing the right ferret for you, there are some things you should be looking for. Choose one that feels right. Ferrets have a variety of personalities, so you should play with several before deciding which one you want.

When we picked out Ralph, we played with him and his sister for about an hour before we made our choice. He seemed to be a little calmer and more interested in people than his sister was. On the other hand, when we first saw our fourth ferret, Knuks, she was extremely nippy and appeared to be frightened of people. But when we realized that the pet shop had been feeding her food she couldn't eat and had been mishandling her, we knew we had to take her home with us. She is now the sweetest and most people-oriented ferret we have. It's amazing what proper care and loving guidance can do for a ferret.

When you go to choose a ferret, you will want to hold him. When you pick him up, make sure you support his whole weight. Dangling a ferret—particularly a bottom-heavy ferret—can put too much stress on his

---

HOW TO HOLD YOUR FERRET

Pick your ferret up with one hand under his front legs, the other supporting his behind. Older males especially may be a little bottom-heavy, and they can be injured if not properly supported.

Another way to hold your ferret is to "scruff" him. This means holding the extra skin at the base of the neck in much the same way a mother cat (or ferret) would carry her young. This is described by many ferret owners as the "off switch." Most ferrets instinctively go limp and relax their muscles (including their mouths) when you grab them in this spot. This is a useful way to restrain your ferret for procedures such as nail clipping, and is not at all painful to your pet. Again, if you have a bottom-heavy ferret, be sure to support his hindquarters.

spine and may injure him. It is best to hold him with one hand under his "arms" and the other under his behind. Of course, it is easy to support the entire weight of a small kit, but as he gets older, you will have to be aware of how you are supporting him.

Ferret-Proofing

Now that you've chosen your ferret, you need to apply yourself to the task of ferret-proofing before you bring your new pet home. Ferret-proofing is unlike proofing your home for any other animal. Ferrets interact with objects as well as people—they like to move things and make things happen. A ferret's small size allows him to get into very small spaces. His abundance of curiosity and determination make off-limits items all the more attractive to him. Often ferret owners set aside a room or two that their ferrets are allowed to play in. Keep in mind that ferret-proofing is never done. Your ferret will constantly be showing you new things that need to be kept out of his reach.

Ferrets are resourceful climbers, so take care to move away objects that can be used as "steps."

Since ferrets are truly domesticated animals, they can survive only a few days outside on their own. Their fearless curiosity usually gets them into trouble even quicker than that. Make sure all screen doors to the outside have sturdy, working latches. Make sure any window screens are secure so your ferret can't push them out and fall out the window. When you have visitors, make sure they know to watch out for your ferret. We usually keep our ferrets caged when we have friends over who are not ferret owners themselves. This way we don't have to worry about someone inadvertently letting one of our ferrets out or stepping or sitting on one of them.

One of the best starting points in ferret-proofing your home is to lie on the floor on your stomach. Look for any small holes (two inches square) that might lead into the walls or to the outside, and block them securely. Once you've blocked off the holes near the floor, look around the room for anything your ferret could use to climb on. Some ferrets are exceptional climbers, though they are not very good at getting down. Our Sabrina can scale the side of the cage in a flash. We have to make sure that there is nothing harmful on top of the cage and that she cannot get to any other furniture (like a bookcase or desk) from the top of the cage.

One of the most common causes of death in ferrets is intestinal blockage. Many ferrets will eat things they shouldn't: rubber, latex, foam, plastic bags, paper, shoe insoles, foam earplugs. The taste of the object doesn't matter; they seem to like the chewy texture. Any spongy or rubbery item should be removed from the area where the ferrets will be playing. Although some ferrets are more prone than others to eating odd objects, it is best to take the most cautious route. Your ferret's life could depend on it. To complete this part of the ferret-proofing task, watch your ferret very closely when you bring him home. If he seems to take a liking to something that's bad for him, remove it from the room.

FERRET HOUSING REQUIREMENTS

Ferrets can live happily in a cage provided there is plenty of time outside the cage for them to play, exercise, and interact with people and their environment.

Things you'll need to provide a cozy home for your ferret:

Large wire mesh cage

Bedding to place over the floor (not wood chips; use old blankets, towels or another soft material)

Litter box

Water bottle

Extras, like hammocks, tunnels, ramps and other architectural toys

Safe toys

Another common cause of injury and death in ferrets is getting caught in reclining chairs or fold-out couches. If you have a recliner, don't use it when your ferret is out playing. Better still, move it to a room your ferret will not be allowed in.

Another danger of couches and chairs is their stuffing. Ferrets can and do find or make holes in the fabric covering the bottom of couches or chairs. Then they climb up inside their new-found and private hideout. This is dangerous for several reasons. First, your pet might eat the stuffing, leading to an intestinal blockage. Second, if you need to get to your ferret in a hurry, you might not be able to reach him. Third, ferrets in your couch could make a mess. To prevent this, you can nail a board or heavy wire mesh onto the bottom of couches or chairs. Of course, not all ferrets will try to get inside your couch. If you supervise your ferret's play carefully, you can prevent any damage to your ferret or your furniture.

Digging comes naturally to ferrets. To keep your houseplants safe, place stones on the dirt at the base of the plant.

You might bring home a ferret who likes to chew on electrical wires. The best way to avoid a tragedy is to keep electrical cords off the floor and out of your ferret's reach. If this is not possible, you can purchase a type of molding that is used to house the wires so your ferret cannot get to them. Another alternative is to spray the cords (but not the plugs!) with Bitter Apple or Bitter Lime spray. If you use the cream, make sure you rub it in completely or your ferret might swallow a blob of it, which could make him ill. Some ferret owners wrap the cords in aluminum foil, which ferrets generally do not like to chew.

Most ferrets like to dig up plants. This is only natural, because they come from a long line of burrowing animals. Ferret owners have come up with some creative ways to help keep their plants and ferrets living together happily and safely. The first option is to move all plants out of your ferret's reach. This will work unless you have a determined climber or very large potted plants that must stay on the floor. The second option is to place large stones on top of the soil in the plant pot. This will keep your ferret from getting to the dirt. It can also weight down the pot, helping to deter your ferret from knocking it over. Third, you can securely attach wire mesh across the top of the plant pot so your ferret cannot reach the dirt. If you have a particularly persistent ferret, you might want to keep your plants in a no-ferret area of your home.

Make the laundry room and kitchen off-limits to your ferret. Ferrets love to curl up in a warm dryer, but this is extremely dangerous.

Plant digging, although messy, is not as dangerous as plant eating. Some plants are poisonous if eaten (poinsettia, for example) and should be kept away from all pets and children. If your ferret takes a liking to eating plants, treat the plant as you would foam rubber—keep it far away from your ferret.

NO-FERRET ZONES

Perhaps the most dangerous room in your home is the kitchen, with the laundry room coming in second. We don't even allow our ferrets in the kitchen. Ferrets can get under the stove, dishwasher or refrigerator. These appliances often have fans, insulation, wires or pilot lights that can cause fatal injuries to your ferret. Many well-loved pet ferrets have died because they were electrocuted under the stove or were badly cut when a fan under the refrigerator turned on suddenly. Ferrets have been known to drink cleaning solutions like window cleaner. Many more ferrets have died because they fell asleep in the clothes dryer.

How do you prevent these tragedies? Make these rooms "ferret-free" zones. You can use a three-foot high piece of stiff cardboard or a lightweight but rigid wood (e.g., doorskin or pressboard) to block the entrance(s) to your kitchen during ferret playtime. You probably don't want a hard wood barrier because you could get hurt if you accidentally kick it while trying to step over it. A child gate is not recommended—your ferret will only use it as a ladder to get to the other side.

FERRET ESSENTIALS

Your new ferret will need:

Large, wire mesh cage

Old towels or other soft bedding

Water bottle

Food dish

Litter boxes (one for the cage and for every room the ferret will be in)

Safe toys

Travel carrier

Even with these precautions, get into the habit of looking through your laundry before you wash it and always check your dryer before turning it on. Ferrets like to sleep in clothes hampers. Open dryers—especially warm ones on cold days—are an open invitation. Ferrets have gotten closed in refrigerators, dryers, closets, drawers and cabinets; be aware of where your ferret is when you are opening and closing any of these. Before you sit down, check under couch or chair cushions. Check under throw rugs before stepping—that bump under the rug could be your ferret.

Proper Toys

Ferrets love to play and they remain playful their entire lives. Your ferret will prefer some toys to others, but be sure that whatever your ferret wants to play with is safe. Not all toys labeled for ferrets are safe for them. Remember that many manufacturers are just beginning to make toys for our little friends and they don't always have experience with ferrets to determine whether the toy is safe. Most sturdy, heavy rubber toys—such as those for large dogs—are appropriate. Never give your ferret soft latex toys or spongy foam rubber toys. A ferret's teeth are designed for eating meat and can therefore tear apart soft toys easily. Your ferret will likely swallow a piece of rubber and, because a ferret's intestines are extremely narrow, he might end up with an intestinal blockage. Routinely check your ferret's toys for chewed areas. As soon as a toy is damaged—even if it's your ferret's favorite—throw it away. Many homemade toys are greatly loved by ferrets. Most ferrets love to run through cardboard tubes, like those from wrapping paper. As long as your ferret doesn't chew on the cardboard, these can make great toys.

Homemade toys, like this blue-jean tube, are inexpensive and great fun for your ferret.

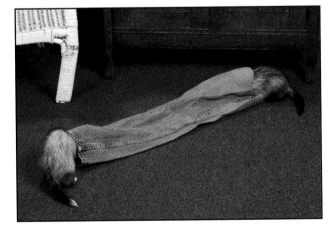

Setting Up the Cage

A ferret should never be kept in a glass aquarium. Ferrets need wire cages similar to those for rabbits or cats. But make sure to cover any wire mesh flooring with linoleum or bedding (towels, blankets) because ferrets should not walk on the open mesh. There are several ferret-specific cages on the market. Some are better than others. As a rule, you should make sure that your ferret has plenty of space, with separate areas for a litter box, food and water and sleeping. Depending on the type of latch on your cage, clips to keep the cage secure might be a good added safety measure. Ferrets can slip through small spaces. Some—especially kits and small females—can squeeze through a latched cage opening. To ensure your ferret doesn't do this, get clips like like those on the end of a leash (available at most fabric or hardware stores) and use them to secure the cage opening. Never underestimate your ferret!

A well set up cage should have a towel on the floor, a litter box on one side, a water bottle and safe toys.

Do not use wood chips in a ferret cage. Cedar and pine chips are treated with oils that can cause your ferret severe respiratory discomfort. There are reports of ferrets taking months to recover from the irritation and damage caused by being kept in wood chips. For the sake of your ferret's health, don't use them. Besides, ferrets are trained to use a litter box (see chapter 8), so there is no need for wood chips.

Hammocks are a favorite sleeping spot for ferrets.

Scruffing mimics the action of the ferret's mother and is not at all uncomfortable for the animal.

FERRET SNOOZE SPOTS

Hammocks are a special favorite of ferrets. They come in many colors and styles and are available in most pet shops. Towels (make sure they aren't frayed or have loops that the ferret might catch his nails on), old sweatshirts or T-shirts, sweat pants or baby blankets are ideal for use as bedding for ferrets. For the first few days especially, check the bedding for any signs that your ferret might be eating it. Some ferrets do eat cloth. If you have a cloth-eater, try using a tightly woven fabric for bedding and leave something in the cage that is appropriate to chew.

44

Additional Supplies

Other items you'll want to pick up before or at the same time you get your ferret: a water bottle or dish, a food dish, litter boxes (one for the cage and at least one in every room your ferret plays in), cat litter, Ferretone or Linatone, Bitter Apple (or Lime) spray (see "Nip Training" in chapter 8), ear cleaning solution, nail clippers, shampoo (see chapter 6), a cat hairball remedy (like Petromalt or Catalax), a harness and leash and a cat carrier. You'll also need to get food for your new friend as discussed in chapter 5.

WATER BOTTLE

Ferrets need to have fresh water all the time. It is best to equip your ferret's cage with a large water bottle, like those made for rabbits or puppies. Change the water in the bottle daily to ensure it is always fresh. When you wash the bottle, be sure to rinse all traces of soap. If the bottle gets too dirty, get a new one. Many ferrets like to lap water from a dish, but many of those same ferrets like to tip over that dish. (Some ferrets even submerge their heads in their water dish.)

Bird dishes that fasten securely to the side of the cage are available in several different styles and will prevent your ferret from dumping his water. You might want to place the water dish directly under the water bottle to catch any drips. A note of caution: We used a bird dish that consisted of a ring that screws onto the cage and a removable metal

Make sure your ferret has plenty of fresh, clean water at all times.

cup. This worked fine with the first three ferrets, but along came Knuks and figured out how to push the cup out of the holder from underneath. The other ferrets didn't appreciate the impromptu bath.

FOOD DISHES

Many ferrets like to dump food dishes, mostly for fun but sometimes to make a point (such as "Pay attention to me!"). The food dish you get for your ferret should be weighted so he can't tip it over. We use a heavy ceramic dog's dish for our business. All four ferrets eat out of the same dish—sometimes at the same time. The bowl you get for your ferret should be large enough to hold plenty of food because ferrets need to have food available to them all the time. Make sure the dish is shallow enough that your ferret can reach the food at the bottom.

LITTER BOX

Most ferret owners train their little friends to use a litter box (see "Litter Training" in chapter 8). There are several ferret-specific litter boxes on the market. Some are designed to fit in the corner of the cage. Some have high sides for ferrets that tend to back up high into corners. Some have one low side to make it easier for your ferret to get in and out. This design is particularly good for older ferrets, who might not be as agile as they once were, or for small kits. Then, of course, there are plain old cat litter boxes that come in various sizes. Any of these are fine to use.

For litter, you will want something that is low-dust. Remember that ferrets are lower to the ground, and therefore closer to the litter in the box, than cats. Also, ferrets—particularly young ones—have a tendency to run their noses through clean litter. Clumping or scoopable litters are not recommended for ferrets because the litter will stick to their noses and get in their eyes. It can also stick to your ferret's fur and rear end, and when he cleans himself he can swallow it. There are several pelletized litters available that are more appropriate for ferrets. Pelletized newspaper is also good.

LEASH AND HARNESS

If you plan on taking your fuzzy outside with you, you will need to get him a harness and leash. The best type of harness is the H-shaped harness. A harness made especially for ferrets will fit much better than a kitten harness cut to fit. As long as you can fit a finger between your ferret and the harness, it is not too tight. Your ferret will get used to wearing the harness fairly quickly. When you put the harness on your ferret he will likely act as if it hurts him or as if he can't walk. It is just that—an act. If you loosen the harness, he'll have it off in seconds. It is very important to fit the harness onto your ferret so he can't get it off. The last thing you want is for him to get out of his harness while you're outside. You can add a little bell to your ferret's harness if you want, but be aware that the bell could get caught on some-thing. Some ferret owners leave the harness on their ferrets all the time and the bell helps them know when the ferret is underfoot.

HOUSEHOLD DANGERS

Ferrets are indoor pets, so you won't need to worry about the danger lurking outside your house. However, there is plenty inside you need to keep your ferret safe from.

electrical cords

cleaning supplies

refrigerator, stove and dishwasher

clothes dryer

houseplants

Ferrets are curious creatures who can get at just about anything. You will always need to be on the look-out for new dangers and escape routes. The task of ferret-proofing is never done.

Although there are ferret collars on the market, we have never had very good luck with them. A ferret's streamlined head and neck make it difficult to get a collar to fit properly or stay on. Most ferrets are pretty good at getting collars off—and hiding them. Some friends have a ferret who has hidden her collar so well, they've given up looking. If you choose to get a collar for your ferret, make sure it fits. Elastic collars are not recommended at all.

TRAVEL CARRIER

You will want to purchase a cat carrier for short trips. The size carrier you get depends on the number of ferrets you have (or plan to have). A small cat carrier is appropriate for one or two ferrets on a short trip. To prevent accidents, you should always put your ferret in a carrier when you travel by car. If you're in a car accident your ferret is more likely to go unharmed if he is in a carrier.

A harness made especially for ferrets is safer and more comfortable than a collar.

Most carriers can be fitted with a small water bottle, and a bird dish for food can be attached to the carrier's door. Many ferret owners use an oblong plastic container as a makeshift litter box for their pet's carrier. If the carrier you purchase is large enough, a small litter box should fit in it.

Now you know all the things you'll need to make your home hospitable to your ferret. Preparing before your ferret arrives will make his arrival less stressful for you and him. You can spend less time and energy scrambling to move things out of the way and concentrate on important things, like getting to know each other.

A ferret can travel easily in a well-equipped travel carrier, though the ferret needs to be inside for it to be truly effective!

chapter 5

Feeding
Your
Ferret

Ferrets are strict carnivores. Their bodies are designed to get the nutrients they require from meat. In the United Kingdom, many working ferrets are fed day-old chicks, which are very high in the meat protein ferrets need. Of course, the average pet owner wants a food that's a little more convenient. Fortunately, there are several high-quality ferret-specific foods on the market today. Ferrets have a short digestive tract, so they need to eat every three to four hours. Your ferret should have food (kibble) and plenty of clean, fresh water available to him at all times.

Nutritional Needs

Because ferrets are carnivores, the food you choose for your ferret must have some form of meat as its first ingredient. Most quality ferret foods on the market list poultry, poultry meal or poultry byproducts as the first ingredient. Foods that list corn or grain as the first ingredient will not provide proper nutrition.

PROTEIN

For years ferret owners fed their little friends high-quality kitten food (growth formula) because it has a high meat protein content. Many owners still feed high-quality kitten food because it is more readily available, and in some cases less expensive, than ferret food. Some ferret enthusiasts feel that kitten food is inappropriate because it is not designed specifically for ferrets. However, others argue that some ferret foods were formulated before animal nutritionists knew much at all about the domestic ferret's needs. This is not a problem with the newer foods formulated specifically for ferrets. Certainly ferrets have thrived on kitten food for many years, and it is better than feeding a poorly formulated ferret diet.

> ### FEEDING YOUR FERRET
>
> Stick to the following guidelines, consult your veterinarian if you have any questions, and feeding your ferret should be an easy task.
>
> - high animal protein and fat content
> - food available all the time
> - plenty of fresh water
> - supplements if needed
> - treats should be healthful and kept to a minimum

In any case, you should *never* feed dog or puppy food to your ferret. Ferrets, like cats, require added taurine, which dog foods do not contain. Taurine is vital to the health of your ferret's eyes and heart. Under no circumstances should you feed your ferret a vegetarian diet. To do so will risk his health.

Why shouldn't ferrets eat vegetable protein? The ferret's digestive tract is like a tube, and food passes through from end to end in about two to four hours. The ferret doesn't have the food in him long enough to extract all the nutrients from vegetables, which have a complex structure. The protein in meat is more readily available and, therefore, the ferret can get what he needs from it within the time he will have the food inside him. The ferret also lacks a cecum, the portion of the digestive tract where vegetable matter is digested. So although vegetable protein isn't necessarily harmful to your ferret, it is inadequate. If you give your ferret too many vegetables as treats, he might go off his regular food, and therefore not get the nutrition he needs.

Ferrets are active, playful animals with an extremely high metabolism. They need to eat every three to four hours.

FAT

Animal fat is another important ingredient in a proper ferret diet. Ferrets get their energy from fat, and will eat enough food to fulfill their energy needs. That means that they will eat less of a food that has high fat content and more of a food that has a lower fat content. Food manufacturers have to make sure that there's enough protein, vitamins and nutrients within the amount of food the ferret will eat. If the percentage of fat in the food is high, the nutrient levels must also be high for the ferret to get a balanced diet. Ferrets, like most other animals except humans, will eat only enough to fulfill their energy needs. They will not overeat.

Fat is also important to the health of your ferret's coat and skin. If you notice your ferret's coat becoming rough or his skin becoming dry, he might benefit from some extra fat in his diet. There are several fatty acid supplements available that you can give him.

SUPPLEMENTS

As a rule, if you feed your ferret a high-quality food, you do not *need* to give him vitamin supplements. Of course, you might *want* to give some vitamin supplements occasionally. Also, if your ferret is ill or under stress, he can benefit from any of a number of vitamin supplements on the market designed specifically for ferrets. One of the most popular types of supplements is an oil-based fatty acid coat and skin vitamin supplement (such as Ferretone), which is similar to Linatone,

a supplement for cats or dogs. There are also vitamin pastes, such as Ferretvite or Nutrical, that ferrets generally regard as treats.

Many of these supplements were designed to make up for deficiencies in the nutrition levels of foods that have since been reformulated. Though the full dose certainly

won't hurt your ferret, many ferret owners feel that it really isn't necessary to give that much as long as your ferret is eating a high-quality food. Even though the bottle suggests coating your ferret's food with Ferretone, this is not recommended. If the coated food remains in the bowl for a few days, or if your ferret stashes the food under the couch, the fat can go bad and might make your ferret sick.

Supplement pastes provide a treat for your ferret as well as oils and vitamins necessary for healthy coat and skin.

We use these supplements as a treat and as a reward in training and teaching tricks (see chapters 8 and 9). This works well since they like the taste and texture of it. Every night we gather all four ferrets and let them lick a teaspoonful or two of Ferretone out of the palms of our hands. This not only gives our ferrets a treat that's good for them, but also gives us a chance to let them know we love them.

Feeding Your Kit

Ferrets do not necessarily need soft foods unless they are ill or very young. The hard food helps keep your ferret's teeth clean. When you first bring home a kit, you will need to soften the food by adding a little water. A young ferret's jaws are not strong enough to break up the hard food. At this early age, you could offer a high-quality canned kitten food in addition to the moistened kibble, but it is not necessary.

It is important that your kit get used to the taste of the kibble, since this is the diet he will eat when he is an adult. As he grows, he will gain the strength he needs to eat hard food. He is usually ready to eat only hard food at the age of twelve to fourteen weeks.

A ferret decides what he considers food while he is still quite young. Beyond this age you might have a hard time convincing him anything is food except what he's already tried. We offered our ferrets a variety of brands of foods when they were young so they wouldn't be too fussy as adults. This is especially important if the only food your ferret likes becomes unavailable. Ferrets who refuse to change foods would rather starve than switch. Many ferret owners have reported that their ferret refused to eat a new food—to the point where they were concerned he would starve to death. Unlike dogs, who will usually eat when they get hungry enough, ferrets have been known to refuse to eat what they don't consider to be food in spite of being hungry. Persistence (also known as stubbornness) is a ferret trait, after all.

Changing Your Ferret's Diet

Never change your ferret's diet suddenly. The best way to switch from one food to another is to do it over the course of about ten days. Start by filling your ferret's dish with a mixture of 10 percent of the new food and 90 percent of his current food. Decrease the percentage of old food by 10 percent as you increase the percentage of new food by 10 percent each day until your ferret's bowl is 100 percent new food.

Gradually switching will help your ferret become accustomed to the new flavor and will give your ferret's body time to adjust to the different nutrient levels. One of the most common side effects of changing foods is diarrhea. No matter what brand you're switching to or from, your ferret will likely have a few loose stools. This is a normal reaction to the dietary change. Once your ferret's body has adjusted, his stool should return to normal. Make sure he drinks plenty of water so he doesn't become dehydrated. Diarrhea can be very serious in an animal as small as a ferret; see chapter 7 for more information about how to treat diarrhea.

Ferrets are social animals who are usually quite happy to share food.

Feeding a Sick Ferret

If your ferret gets sick, he might need a special diet. Ferrets who have stomach ulcers need to be on a bland diet, just like people who have ulcers. Ferrets recovering from surgery need a food that's easy to digest. Any of a variety of illnesses can make your ferret go off his food. But ferrets are small and need to keep up their strength when they are sick. How can you get your ferret to eat when he doesn't feel like eating?

"Duck Soup"

The answer is "Duck Soup." There is no definitive recipe for Duck Soup. Usually it is a soft mixture of your ferret's regular food moistened (you can

moisten it with an electrolyte replacer, like Pedialyte), chicken or turkey baby food, Sustacal or Ensure (soy-based), and Ferretvite or Nutrical. Sometimes canned kitten food is added. Basically, Duck Soup is a high-calorie, good-tasting, liquid mix of foods that your ferret is more likely to eat than his regular food.

If your ferret is sick enough to need Duck Soup, you might need to force-feed him. Force-feeding is really not forceful at all. If you must put the food in your ferret's mouth for him, do so very carefully. You do not want him to choke on the food or have the food enter his windpipe. Often, putting a dab on his nose will

Healthy treats in small amounts are useful for training and showing your ferret how much you love him.

make him lick off the food. If you use an eye-dropper, place the food at the front of your ferret's mouth or into his cheek (as you would for a human infant). Put only a tiny amount of food in his mouth at a time. If you are uncomfortable force-feeding your ferret, talk to your veterinarian. He will be able to show you the proper way to feed your sick ferret.

Treats

Giving your ferret treats is a good opportunity to create a bond between you and your pet. Often, the only time a young ferret will sit still long enough for you to hold him is when you are giving him a treat. But remember, no treat should keep your ferret from eating his regular food. The most important thing to remember about treats is that they are just that—treats. Anything you feed your ferret that is not his regular diet should be kept to a minimum.

Most ferrets love raisins, but giving them more than one or two a day will give them diarrhea. Also, there's quite a bit of sugar in raisins, and too much sugar is not good for your ferret. To make raisins last longer, break them into halves or quarters—your ferret will think he's pulled one over on you. Your ferret might also like a variety of fruits and vegetables like bananas, melon, peppers, papaya or apple. You should be particularly careful with these because they don't have usable nutrition for ferrets. Some more nutritious types of treats are cooked beef, cooked chicken (or chicken livers), hard-boiled eggs or other types of cooked meat. You will also find several brands of ferret treats at the pet store. Some ferrets also like low-sugar, low-salt cereals like Cheerios or Kix. These, too, should be kept to a bare minimum because what's low sugar for you and me is pretty high sugar for a little ferret.

Foods Your Ferret Shouldn't Have

Ferrets, like children, tend to most like the things that are worst for them. Sugar or anything with sugar in it, for example, is well-loved by our fuzzy friends. But ferrets can't process sugars very well—not even natural sugars. Keeping your ferret off the sweets is your best bet. Ferrets also tend to like alcoholic beverages, which contain very high amounts of sugar. You should never allow your ferret to drink beer or wine or anything with alcohol in it.

More "don'ts": nuts, dairy and chocolate. Ferrets can't digest nuts, and if your ferret swallows a large enough piece, he can end up with an intestinal blockage. Some ferrets love peanut butter, which is okay as a treat, as long as it is smooth peanut butter, not chunky. Dairy foods will cause diarrhea in ferrets. Chocolate can be toxic to ferrets and other animals. Although ferrets have stolen and eaten a bit of chocolate with no adverse effect, it is not worth the risk.

Basically, try to remember that ferrets are small, and even small amounts of things like sugar, alcohol or dairy foods can be hard for them to digest and may make them sick. Stick to the nutritious treats; your ferret will thank you for it.

Grooming
Your
Ferret

Good grooming is not just a matter of making your pet look pretty. Keeping your ferret's ears and teeth clean and his nails trimmed will help keep him healthy and happy. You should set up a regular grooming routine for your ferret that includes bathing and brushing (especially during shedding season), nail clipping, ear cleaning and checking teeth for tartar buildup.

Bath Time

How often you should bathe your ferret depends on who you ask. Some owners swear by bathing once every two to four weeks. Others insist that ferrets need not be bathed unless they actually get dirt on them (from, say, rolling in the mud or digging in a just-watered plant). Whatever works best for you is fine, but don't bathe your ferret more often than every two weeks. Frequent washing strips away essential oils, leaving your ferret's fur coarse and his skin dry, and generally making him very uncomfortable.

There are several ferret-specific shampoos on the market you can use to wash your ferret. You can also use a baby-safe shampoo or, as some ferret owners recommend, an all-natural peppermint soap bought at a health food store. If your ferret has fleas, you can use a flea shampoo that is safe for kittens. Never use flea dips on your ferret; they are too harsh.

Bathing your ferret can be easy. You can bathe him in a kitchen or bathroom sink, in the bathtub or in any basin. Make sure the room is fairly warm and there are no drafts. We wash ours in the kitchen sink. If you have double sinks in the kitchen, so much the better. You can use one for washing and one for rinsing.

Some ferrets prefer taking showers—it seems to be less threatening for them. There are owners who bring their ferrets into the shower (or bathtub) with them to help make

You can bathe your ferret in warm water in the kitchen sink.

the ferret feel more comfortable. If you have a ferret who likes water, he might try to hop into the shower any chance he gets. Just be sure to warn houseguests if your ferret likes showers. It can be disturbing to suddenly feel a little tongue lapping at your ankle when you thought you were in the shower alone.

Your ferret's body temperature is normally 101 to 102 degrees Fahrenheit, so a "lukewarm" bath can feel pretty cold to him. (That's why he races up your arm and tries to leap off of you—it's cold!) The water should be about as warm as a bath for a child—not too hot, but comfortable. Warming the shampoo bottle in the bath water beforehand can add to your ferret's comfort. Don't overfill the sink. The water should reach only up to your ferret's shoulders, so he can stand in the water without feeling that he has to swim. Keep in mind that while some ferrets love the water, many only tolerate it, and some are simply terrified. Be patient and offer treats for good behavior. The more pleasant you make your ferret's bathing experience, the easier it will be on both of you.

When wetting down your ferret, make sure you support his weight. Apply the shampoo carefully and avoid getting it in his eyes. Most ferrets like the taste of soap and shampoo, but you should try to keep them from eating it. Don't panic if your fuzzy gets a little lick of shampoo; a *tiny* bit won't harm him. After lathering up, make sure you rinse. And rinse. And rinse. Leaving shampoo residue on your ferret can make his fur rough and his skin dry, which can be very uncomfortable for him.

Make sure you dry your ferret thoroughly before he heads to the dustiest place in the house!

Make sure your ferret has a clean place to dry off. Ferrets tend to head for the dustiest, dirtiest places to rub against to get dry, undoing any washing you have done. A dry bathtub or other confined area filled with towels for your freshly washed ferret to burrow through is a fun way to dry off. You might want to warm the towels in the clothes dryer first—but don't let them get too hot. Some ferrets will tolerate being blown dry. If you choose to do this, be careful. Choose a warm—not hot—setting, keep the blow dryer at least twelve

inches away from your ferret, and move the blow dryer frequently to prevent burns. Wherever or however you

dry your ferret, make sure the room is warm and has
no drafts.

Brushing Your Ferret

Particularly during shedding seasons (spring and fall),
you may want to brush your ferret to help remove
loose fur. (Ferrets get furballs. More on those in chapter 7.) Choose a brush for cats or kittens, keeping in
mind that your ferret's fur is not as long as some cats'
fur. We use a medium-bristle cat brush on ours when
they need it. When brushing your ferret, be sure to use
even pressure—some ferrets are a bit ticklish and will
squirm to get away. If your ferret gets fleas, use a flea
comb to remove the flea dirt.

Clipping Nails

Keeping your ferret's nails trimmed is an important
part of his grooming program. Regular nail trimming
will prevent your ferret
from getting his nails
caught on carpeting or
bedding. Your ferret
will need to have his
nails clipped about every
two weeks, some more,
some less. Ferrets tend
to wear down their back
claws quicker than their
front claws, so you may
need to clip the nails
on the front paws more
frequently.

A ferret's nails are similar in structure to a
dog's nails; they do not

*Brush your fer-
ret during shed-
ding seasons to
help remove loose
fur.*

retract like a cat's claws. Your ferret's claws are important to proper balance and walking. If your ferret's
nails get too long, his toes will not rest properly on
the ground, and his gait will be affected. Because the
ferret's claws are not retractable, you cannot declaw
a ferret without removing part of the toe. Declawing

is not recommended, and most veterinarians will not perform this procedure because it is considered mutilation. If your ferret digs at the carpet, try spraying Bitter Apple or Lime on the area he scratches, or place a plastic runner on the area. (A couple of ferret owners who have particularly persistent carpet diggers have given up on carpeting altogether and have bare floors instead.)

THE CLIPPING PROCEDURE

The easiest way to clip your ferret's nails is to put a drop or two of Ferretone (or other "lickable" treat) on his belly. While the ferret is licking the treat, he will not notice that you are clipping his nails.

You can use a cat nail clipper or a human nail clipper to trim your ferret's nails. Some ferret owners feel that human clippers tend to crush the nail before cutting it; making sure the clippers are sharp minimizes this concern. Other ferret owners feel that cat clippers obstruct the view of the nail. Use whichever type of clipper you feel most comfortable with.

Once you have chosen the type of clipper you will use and have prepared your ferret's belly, you're ready to start trimming. While your ferret is licking the treat, gently spread apart the toes on each foot, in turn, and clip the nails. Try to clip the nail so the tip will be parallel with the floor. Avoid clipping the quick (the pinkish-red vein inside the nail), because it will bleed. If you do clip it by mistake, put styptic powder on the nail. If you have no styptic, you can put the ferret's nail in cold water or run the nail across a bar of white soap to stop the bleeding. You may want to resume the nail clipping later in the day to give your ferret some time to calm down.

Regular nail trimming will prevent your ferret from catching his nails on carpet or bedding.

63

If your ferret's nails have not been clipped for a long time, the quick will grow long. In this case, you may need to trim the nail several times over the course of two weeks. The quick will recede away from the nail tip after you clip the nail. Once it has receded, you can clip a little more of the nail.

Cleaning Ears

Cleaning a ferret's ears can be a real challenge, but it must be done. If you don't clean your ferret's ears, they become a breeding ground for mites. Left untreated for a long period of time, ear mites can cause severe damage to a ferret's ear drums and the delicate bones of the inner ear, leading to infections and possibly deafness. If you suspect your ferret has ear mites (a dark brown or black discharge that looks like coffee grounds, scratching at ears), have him examined by your veterinarian.

Ferrets' ears tend to produce a lot of ear wax and can be breeding grounds for mites, so you must clean them thoroughly and consistently.

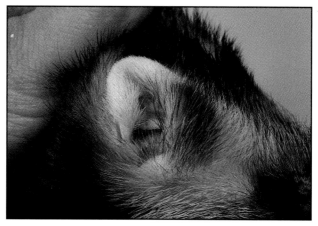

Ferrets tend to produce a lot of ear wax. But different ferrets produce different amounts, and even the same ferret can produce varying amounts of ear wax at different times. Normal ear wax is usually reddish or light brown in color. It has a distinct odor that many people find objectionable. Keeping your ferret's ears clean will minimize this odor.

The hardest part of ear cleaning is that ferrets usually don't like it. You will probably need someone to help you hold your ferret still. Many breeders and seasoned ferret owners can scruff the ferret with one hand and clean the ears with the other. Ear cleaning takes a little practice, but don't give up. This is a very important part of grooming your ferret.

You can use any ear-cleaning solution that is considered safe for kittens. Many of the all-natural ear-cleaning solutions are fine as well. Keep in mind that the inside of your ferret's ears are sensitive and must be moistened in order to be cleaned. Do not use a dry cotton swab.

A good method—and the one we use—is to wet down one end of a cotton swab with ear-cleaning solution, swab the ferret's ear (never go into the ear canal, go only as far as you can see), and use the dry end of the swab to remove dirt, wax and excess moisture. Ferrets have a little "pouch" at the back of the ear which can collect a good amount of dirt and wax. Make sure you clean this pouch thoroughly. It is not the ear canal, so you can slip the cotton swab in and out without causing any damage. And always, always be gentle.

FERRET GROOMING ESSENTIALS

Shampoo

Cat or kitten brush

Cat or human nail clipper

Cotton swabs

Ear cleaning solution

Gauze

Cleaning Teeth

Your ferret's teeth accumulate tartar just as any other animal's do. Unfortunately, many owners overlook their ferret's dental health. Gum disease—characterized by red, inflamed gums—can lead to severe discomfort and infection. A decayed or abscessed tooth can make your ferret go off his food and lead to serious infection and even death. It is important that your ferret always have hard food to help keep his teeth clean. In addition, your veterinarian should periodically perform a complete dental exam and service on your ferret, including removal of tartar on the ferret's teeth and above the gum line. Most ferrets need this full procedure after they reach about three or four years old.

Tartar is a gray or greenish discoloration on your ferret's teeth. Usually it is seen first on the back teeth. If any of your ferret's teeth is a brownish color, there is a possibility of decay. Have your vet check it out as soon as possible.

If you start when your ferret is young, you can get him used to having his teeth cleaned fairly easily. Although nothing takes the place of a professional tooth cleaning, there are some things you can do to help keep your ferret in good dental health. Between tooth cleanings or from the time your ferret is young, you can use a cat toothbrush or wrap ordinary gauze around your finger and "brush" his teeth on a weekly basis. It will take some time for your ferret to get used to this, so be patient and gentle. Always offer a reward for good behavior. *Never* use human toothpaste on your ferret; the ingredients (especially fluoride) are poisonous when swallowed, and ferrets can't

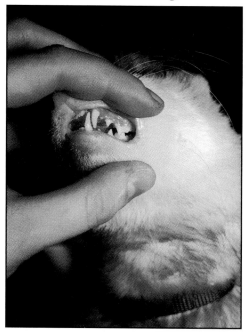

Check your ferret's teeth frequently for tartar and discoloration. This ferret has clean teeth and pink gums—signs of good oral health.

spit it out. Besides, most ferrets hate the smell and taste of it. If your ferret will tolerate it, you can use a toothpaste specially formulated for cats. The more important part of brushing is the abrasiveness of the gauze, which helps take off the tartar while it is relatively soft, so toothpaste is really not needed. Your ferret might tolerate the brushing better if you put a drop of Ferretone or Linatone on the gauze.

In some cases, you can remove superficial tartar from your ferret's teeth yourself by scratching at the tartar with your fingernail. Often the tartar will pop off in fragments. If you are the least bit uncomfortable scraping tartar from your ferret's teeth, don't do it. Instead, have your vet clean your ferret's teeth. Some experienced ferret owners do an abbreviated form of tartar removal on their ferret's teeth when it is absolutely necessary, using a dental instrument for the scraping and following up by "polishing" the teeth with gauze. This takes a good amount of practice, and can lead to injury if you slip and cut the ferret's gums. Again, do only what you're comfortable doing. A little tartar buildup is better than injured gums and a traumatized ferret.

A well-groomed ferret is a thing of beauty.

Close attention to coat, nails, ears and teeth helps you keep your ferret looking and feeling his best. Grooming your ferret gives you an opportunity to recognize potential problems and prevent them before they start. In addition, keeping your ferret clean makes him a pleasure to be around. In short, a well-groomed ferret is truly a thing of beauty.

chapter 7

Keeping Your Ferret
Healthy

Finding a veterinarian to properly care for your ferret can be much more difficult than finding one for your dog or cat. Most, if not all, veterinary schools classify the ferret as an exotic animal. As such, veterinary students are not necessarily required to learn about ferrets. Often courses that cover exotic animals in general do not go into depth about any one animal. What does this mean to you? It means that before you take your new ferret for his first visit, you need to ask your veterinarian if he or she has experience with ferrets. If not, ask if he or she can refer you to one who does. Often a local ferret shelter/rescue, ferret club or reputable pet shop will be able to put you in touch with a good ferret vet in your area.

Finding a Veterinarian

Ferrets have special veterinary needs. Many ferret-specific diseases may be misdiagnosed by veterinarians without ferret experience, resulting in unfortunate consequences. We changed vets several times until we found one with whom we were happy. Take the time to find a vet with whom you and your ferret are comfortable. Don't be afraid to ask questions about how many ferrets the veterinarian sees weekly and what types of ferret medical problems he or she has treated. Look into emergency-care veterinarians who personally provide twenty-four-hour service as well. The last thing you want to do is start looking for a ferret-knowledgeable veterinarian at 2 A.M. when your ferret needs medical attention. The footwork you do up front can help save time and your ferret's life in an emergency.

Find a veterinarian who has had experience treating ferrets before you have to deal with an emergency situation.

Your new ferret kit will need to visit the veterinarian a day or two after you bring him home. Usually during this visit he will be checked for any parasites (like ear mites) and for overall health. He'll also receive a vaccination for canine distemper (see below). Be sure to bring a stool sample so your vet can check for intestinal parasites.

Vaccinations

If you bring home an adult ferret and you do not know or cannot find out his vaccination status, you will need to have him vaccinated. In these cases, it is recommended that the ferret receive two distemper vaccinations three weeks apart and yearly boosters thereafter. The ferret should also receive a rabies vaccination.

As with any vaccination, there is always the rare chance of an adverse reaction. Remember to stay at your vet's office for at least thirty minutes after your ferret receives a shot, and keep an eye on your ferret for twenty-four hours after that. If you notice any kind of reaction (vomiting, diarrhea or seizure, for example), take your ferret back to the vet immediately. Our ferrets are usually a little sleepy after a vet visit and vaccination. After his most recent vaccination, Marshmallow developed a red spot at the injection site, but was otherwise all right. Sometimes a lump can develop at the injection site, but this is nothing to worry about. Recently, some veterinarians have recommended leaving two weeks between the canine distemper and rabies vaccinations in an attempt to minimize vaccine reactions. There are arguments in favor of and against this practice; you should do what you and your vet are most comfortable with.

Take your kit to the veterinarian for an overall health check and vaccinations within two days of bringing him home.

Just because your ferret has had a bad reaction doesn't necessarily mean that he can never be vaccinated again. Many veterinarians will give an antihistamine to a ferret that has had a reaction in the past to help prevent the reaction from occurring again. You will have to weigh the risk of the disease (keeping in mind that canine distemper is fatal to ferrets) against the risk of a serious reaction to the vaccine. Discuss the possible options with your veterinarian.

CANINE DISTEMPER

Ferrets are susceptible to canine distemper (not feline distemper, as was once believed), a viral infectious disease that affects the respiratory, gastrointestinal and neurological systems. This disease is fatal and it is airborne, so you can bring it in on your clothes. You must vaccinate your ferret against canine distemper. Usually the breeder, whether private or one of the large breeder farms, has given the kit his first canine distemper vaccination. A kit receives a canine distemper vaccination at six to eight weeks of age and every three to four weeks afterward until he is fourteen weeks of age, and then yearly boosters thereafter. Usually, your ferret will get one distemper shot at the first vet visit and another shot three or four weeks later.

> **EMERGENCY WARNING SIGNS**
>
> If you notice any of these symptoms, get in touch with your veterinarian as soon as possible.
>
> Severe and sudden loss of appetite
>
> Green or yellow nasal discharge
>
> Profuse diarrhea
>
> Repeated vomiting

RABIES

Whether or not your ferret goes outside, he should be vaccinated against rabies. It may be required by law in your area. In any event, if your ferret bites someone, having up-to-date rabies vaccinations can be reassuring and often can help dissuade the person from reporting the bite, keeping your ferret from being killed and tested for the virus. (See chapter 11 for more about departments of health and rabies.) Most important, keeping your ferret's rabies vaccination current protects him if he comes in contact with a rabid animal. The only USDA-approved rabies vaccine for ferrets is Imrab-3. Your ferret should receive his first rabies vaccination at approximately fourteen to sixteen weeks (older than three months) of age, and yearly boosters thereafter.

Neutering

The vast majority of ferrets bought in pet shops come from large breeder farms that alter (spay or castrate) and descent the animals before they even reach the store. Because the surgery is performed when they are very young, there will be no physical indication that the surgery has been performed (that is, the fur will be grown in and you will not see a scar). However, ferrets from large breeder farms usually have a tattoo in one of their ears, which indicates that the ferret has been neutered. If you get your ferret from a private breeder, you will need to have her spayed (or him castrated) by the time she reaches six or seven months old. The breeder should give you the information you need, and recommend a veterinarian who can perform the surgery. If the breeder doesn't offer this information, ask.

Pet ferrets must be neutered. Female ferrets (jills) will not come out of heat on their own. Prolonged heat will lead to serious medical problems and, eventually, death. Male ferrets (hobs) cycle into "rut," which, for our purposes, can be described as something like a female's heat cycle. When a hob is in rut, he is aggressive toward other male ferrets (not people), even males that have been neutered. Also, hobs in rut have a very strong, unpleasant odor and they can undergo dramatic weight changes and suffer anxiety if they are not bred.

Breeding ferrets is not easy. Often the jills don't produce enough milk for their litters. They can also get serious infections. Some jills are not good mothers and will hurt or kill their kits. Besides the health concerns, indiscriminate breeding can lead to overpopulation. On the whole, it is best by far to leave breeding to the professionals.

Emergency Care and First Aid

It is always better to prevent illness and injury than to try to cure or fix things afterward. That's why we have our pets vaccinated and why we bring them to the vet for annual checkups. But despite even our best efforts, our ferrets can get into trouble and get hurt. Illnesses can be cured more easily if they're diagnosed and treated early, and the damage can be kept to a minimum if you know the correct first aid. Many common problems for ferrets are listed below along with symptoms and, where appropriate, remedies. This is not an exhaustive list and is not meant to take the place of solid veterinary advice. In any case, if you are unsure of what to do or whether your ferret is ill, seek the advice of your veterinarian. Remember that ferrets are small and have quick metabolisms; it is always better to go to the vet than to wait to see if your ferret improves.

Some symptoms that might seem to indicate a problem are really just normal ferret behaviors. Read chapter 3 to gain a better understanding of some normal ferret behaviors like shivering, deep sleep and itching.

One of the challenges in dealing with an injured ferret is that ferrets—even when they are hurt—are not likely to want to sit still. Often, an injured ferret will have to be immobilized for his own safety. Remember that your ferret may be frightened or in pain. Even if you must hold him tightly, be gentle and speak to him in a reassuring tone. Try to call your veterinarian before you leave your home so he is ready to see your ferret as soon as you arrive.

Bleeding

If your ferret is bleeding, apply pressure to the wound and go to the vet. A ferret tends to ignore pain until it is extreme, and while he may not be acting any differently, he may have internal injuries you are unaware of.

If your ferret is bleeding as a result of clipping the nail quick (which is not uncommon), it can usually be stopped by applying styptic powder. If you don't have styptic powder, you can use cornstarch or flour, or you can press your ferret's toe into a bar of soap. If the nail is torn off higher (at the nail base), he will need veterinary attention. Do not dab at the toe or put pressure directly on the wound. This will only interfere with the natural clotting process. Instead, try to stop the bleeding by applying pressure above the toes. Take your ferret to the vet.

Broken Bone

If you suspect your ferret has broken a bone, try to keep him from moving around and go to your vet. Often confining your ferret to a small carrier or wrapping him in a towel will keep him from moving around too much. Do not try to splint your ferret's legs. If you have stepped on or sat on your ferret, keep him immobilized (in a small carrier or wrapped in a towel) and take him to the vet. If your ferret takes a bad fall or is dropped, take him to the vet even if he seems all right.

Spinal Injury

The ferret's spine is long and allows him to twist into some unusual positions. It might look like your ferret is infinitely flexible, but he is not. Never swing your ferret around, and always support all of his weight. However, accidents can happen. If you suspect your ferret has a spinal injury, try to keep him as still as possible and go to the vet immediately.

Animal Bite

If your ferret is bitten by another animal, put pressure on the wound and take him to the veterinarian. Remember to tell your vet that your ferret has been bitten, especially if your ferret has been bitten by an unknown, stray or wild animal. If possible, find out if the animal that bit your ferret is up to date on its rabies vaccination.

Poisoning

If your ferret drinks or eats something poisonous to him (including human medications, cleaning solutions, alcoholic beverages etc.), find the container the substance was in and take it and your ferret to your veterinarian. If your ferret seems all right and ate or drank only a small amount, you can call the National

Animal Poison Control Center (a nonprofit organization) at (900) 680-0000 ($20 for the first five minutes, plus $2.95 for each additional minute) or (800) 548-2423 ($30 per case; credit cards only) to find out the best way to proceed. Different poisonous substances must be treated in different ways; make sure you consult a professional.

Try to keep poisonous substances well out of your ferret's reach. If he does ingest something dangerous, call your veterinarian immediately.

Electric Shock

If your ferret gets shocked as a result of chewing on an electrical wire, you should wrap him in a blanket to keep him warm and bring him to the vet.

Broken Tooth

A chipped or broken tooth is not necessarily a problem for your ferret. It becomes a problem if the root is exposed or if the tooth begins to decay. If you notice that your ferret's tooth is turning brown or that he is favoring one side of his mouth, take him to the vet. A decaying tooth can lead to other problems, including gum disease and abscesses.

Heat Stroke

This condition results from increased temperatures and is possible at temperatures above 80 degrees Fahrenheit. If your ferret exhibits symptoms of heat stroke (panting, severe lethargy, limpness, seizures and, eventually, unconsciousness), you will need to decrease your ferret's body temperature steadily, but not suddenly. You can apply cool (*not* cold) water over your ferret, concentrating on the feet and groin areas. You can also apply rubbing alcohol to your ferret's feet only (not his whole body). Be careful not to bring his temperature too far down. Give him water if he will drink on his own. Then you should bring your ferret to the vet even if he seems all right. He might need fluid replacement and further care. It is always best to prevent heat stroke. Do not leave your ferret in a car for any amount of time during summer months. Keep him out of direct sunlight and make sure that he always has plenty of fresh water.

Ferrets can get shocked by chewing on exposed electrical cords. Secure these out of your ferret's reach.

Diarrhea

Because ferrets are small animals, diarrhea can become life-threatening if not treated quickly. Diarrhea can occur as a result of stress, dietary indiscretion (like eating one raisin too many), foreign body obstruction, gastrointestinal irritation, liver disease, coccidiosis or toxicity. It could also be due to a bacterial, parasitic or viral infection (see "Epizootic Catarrhal Enteritis," below).

Another possible, though uncommon, cause of diarrhea is proliferative bowel disease, which occurs especially in young ferrets. The general rule is: If your ferret has more than two loose stools, take him to the vet and bring a sample of the stool with you. Your vet will be better able to diagnose and treat the cause of the diarrhea if he can examine the stool. Prolonged or repeated bouts of diarrhea can lead to dehydration and death.

Dehydration

You can tell if your ferret is dehydrated by gently scruffing him. If the skin stays pinched, he is dehydrated. If the skin snaps back, he is all right. You should observe how quickly your ferret's skin snaps back when he is healthy so you will be able to tell whether he is dehydrated when he is sick.

To treat diarrhea, make sure your ferret drinks plenty of water or electrolyte replacer (like Pedialyte or Gatorade). If he refuses to drink, use an eyedropper to feed him fluids. Place the eyedropper in the corner of your ferret's mouth, between his lips and teeth, and slowly drip the water into your ferret's mouth. You must do this slowly or your ferret might inhale the water. For a two-pound ferret, you can give about 0.5 cc (0.5 ml) of Kaopectate every four hours.

Vomiting

This can be a sign of a serious illness. If your ferret vomits more than once or twice and is not able to keep food down, take him to the veterinarian immediately. Vomiting is one of the primary signs of intestinal blockage, which is fatal if not treated. See "Intestinal Blockage" below.

Many illnesses can become serious quickly in your ferret because of his small size. Whenever your ferret is under the weather, keep a close eye on him. If he seems to be getting worse, don't hesitate to take him to the vet.

Common Diseases and Conditions

Recognizing many of these illnesses depends on close observation of your ferret. The more interaction you have with your ferret, the better you will know his usual behavior and the better you will be able to know when he is not acting normally. In the ferret, many illnesses are diagnosed and cured by surgery. In cases like intestinal blockages, your vet might want to do an exploratory surgery. During the procedure, he can check out the health of other organs, and catch possible problems sooner. Although any surgery is serious, it has become much safer since most veterinarians have begun to routinely use a general anesthetic called Isoflurane. Your vet should not use any other general anesthetic on your ferret.

ADRENAL DISEASE

Hyperadrenocorticoidism most often occurs in ferrets three years of age or older. It is sometimes misdiagnosed as Cushing's disease (which ferrets do not get). These are symptoms to watch for:

- Hair loss beginning at the base of the tail (not the tip) and progressing up the spine (some ferrets will be totally bald before the problem is diagnosed)

- Flaky, red and inflamed skin that is sometimes overly itchy (ferrets are a bit itchy to begin with, but the hormone secreted by these growths can cause excessive itching)

- Lethargy

- In females (even if they're spayed), a swollen vulva; in males, aggressive sexual (mounting) behavior even if they have been neutered

If your ferret has these symptoms, you should take him to the veterinarian. Most veterinarians will diagnose adrenal disease based on the collection of symptoms outlined above. Conventional tests (x-ray, ultrasound, blood tests) cannot be used to rule out adrenal disease, meaning that your ferret can have adrenal disease even if the test doesn't show it. The best treatment for adrenal disease is surgery to remove the affected gland. After surgery, the symptoms will begin to abate (vulva returns to normal size within a day or so). The ferret's fur will grow back, usually within six months. Ferrets that have an adrenal gland removed can go on to live happy, healthy and long lives.

BLINDNESS (CATARACTS)

Many authorities agree that ferret eyesight isn't very good to begin with. Ferrets that are blind do all right despite their limitation. Ferrets are very adaptable creatures with a true zest for life, and they don't let a little blindness get in their way. It is important to be extra gentle and careful around a ferret with limited or no vision. Most commonly the cause of blindness is cataracts, though it can also be an inherited trait. A cataract has a milky white, often opaque, discoloration within the pupil. If you notice a cataract in your ferret's eye, you should bring it to the attention of your veterinarian.

CARDIOMYOPATHY

Cardiomyopathy is the progressive deterioration of the heart muscles, and most often occurs in ferrets over three years old. Symptoms include difficulty waking up, the need to rest during playtime and a general decrease in activity or collapse. As the disease advances, there is coughing and difficulty breathing and increased respiration rate. Because cardiomyopathy usually occurs in older ferrets who are slowing down a little anyway, it is often overlooked. Although there is no cure for cardiomyopathy, your veterinarian can prescribe treatment.

If your ferret is less active and seems to tire more easily than usual, have his heart checked by your veterinarian.

DEAFNESS

Deafness, like blindness, doesn't seem to present much of a problem for ferrets. Our Ralph is deaf and gets along just fine. One of the concerns with a deaf ferret is that he will not hear a squeak toy or bell if you are trying to call him. Deafness has been associated with white coat color (or variants thereof) in ferrets as well as many other species, including cats.

DESCENTING

Ferrets have scent glands all over their bodies. When a ferret is described as "descented," it means that the anal sacs have been removed. The ferret can express this gland at will, like its cousin the skunk. However, the odor from the gland is not as strong or as lingering as that of a skunk. Many ferret owners argue that descenting a ferret is unnecessary. In some European countries, such as Germany, descenting a ferret with healthy anal scent glands is an illegal procedure because it is considered mutilation. Many veterinarians will attempt to dissuade a ferret owner from descenting an adult ferret. In general, ferrets who are neutered early in life are also descented. If you get a ferret from a breeder and wait until the ferret is six months old before neutering, descenting is not really necessary. The sex hormones level out as a result of neutering, which greatly reduces the productivity of the scent glands.

EAR MITES

Ear mites are a common problem in ferrets. Many kits pick them up on their journey from breeder to pet shop to your home, which is why it is very important to have your vet check your ferret's ears during the initial visit. Your vet can look at the ear wax under a microscope. Ear mites are easily treated with ear drops from your veterinarian. Keeping your ferret's ears clean is the best way to prevent ear mites (see chapter 6 for how to clean ears), but even ferrets whose ears are cleaned regularly can get mites when you add a new ferret to the group.

Ear mites spread easily, so if you have more than one ferret, you will likely have to treat all your ferrets. Make sure you follow through with the treatment your vet prescribes. You will also want to clean the ferret's cage thoroughly and bathe the ferret using a kitten-safe flea shampoo. Suspect ear mites if your ferret's ear wax is dark brown or black (as opposed to reddish) and if there's more of it than usual. Sometimes you can see movement if you place a swab of the wax from your ferret's ear on a piece of white paper. This is not a foolproof way to tell if your ferret has ear mites. Make sure your vet checks it out.

Epizootic Catarrhal Enteritis (ECE)

This viral infection, commonly called "Green Diarrhea," "Green Slime" or "The Greenies," affects the lining of the intestine, which causes profuse mucous diarrhea. Often the diarrhea varies from bright to olive green. Diarrhea of any kind is a serious matter in ferrets because they are small and can become dehydrated quickly. ECE is very contagious. It is transmitted via direct contact, but you can also carry the virus on your clothes to your ferret. Researchers believe ferrets shed the virus (remain contagious) for at least six months after the episode. The only way to prevent your ferret from getting ECE is to keep him away from any other ferrets or ferret owners. If you go to a place where there are ferrets or ferret owners (like a

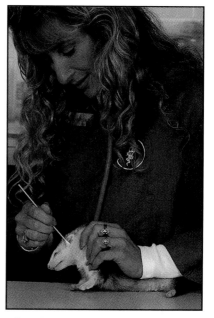

ferret show), you risk bringing the virus home to your ferret. Keeping your ferret isolated is the best way to prevent ECE. Some people in the ferret community believe that treating it like an inevitable childhood disease is the best approach, exposing the ferret while he is young and better able to fight the virus. ECE causes a long-lasting immunity following exposure. However, some ferrets may be more prone to getting diarrhea whenever they are sick after they have had ECE.

If your ferret's ear wax appears dark brown or black, have the vet check for ear mites.

If your ferret becomes sick with ECE you will have to treat it aggressively. Make sure your ferret continues to drink and eat. At the first signs, start giving your ferret an electrolyte replacer such as Pedialyte. Feeding an easily digestible diet like Duck Soup (see chapter 5 for the recipe) will help keep up your ferret's strength and help to keep him hydrated. A visit to your veterinarian for antibiotics is often a good idea. Although the antibiotics will not cure the ECE, they will help to prevent your ferret from getting secondary infections that he will be more susceptible to because he has been weakened by the diarrhea.

If you notice your ferret becoming dehydrated, you will need to bring him to the vet to have fluids given subcutaneously or intravenously. Because ECE is a virus, it has to run its course. The best you can do for your ferret is make sure he stays hydrated and continues to get some nutrients. ECE is a more serious concern in older ferrets or otherwise ill ferrets.

FLEAS

Because ferrets are not outdoor pets like dogs or cats, many escape the problem of fleas and ticks. However, if you have a dog or a cat, he can bring these in from outside. Fleas can be a real problem for ferrets. The old reliable flea shampoo is a good first line of defense. Never use a flea dip on your ferret; flea shampoos for kittens (in which the active ingredients are pyrethrins) are recommended. Make sure you rinse your ferret completely. Treating the environment is just as important as treating your pet, so be sure to wash all your ferret's bedding. Because some ferrets are actually allergic to fleas, it is a good idea to keep an eye out for any particularly severe reactions. If you suspect your ferret is allergic, bring him to the vet.

If you use a flea bomb in your home, make sure you and your pets will not be home for several hours. Be sure to vacuum and wipe down all surfaces thoroughly before letting your fuzzy run around again. Remember that they are low to the ground and their fur will pick up anything your vacuum cleaner misses.

To help repel fleas, some pet owners recommend giving brewer's yeast at the dose recommended for a cat. However, some veterinarians question the effectiveness of brewer's yeast in repelling fleas. You can also talk to your vet about the flea pill, Program, which some vets have been giving to ferrets at the cat dosage. Never put a flea collar on your ferret; it is too harsh for him.

GASTROINTESTINAL ULCERS

Stomach ulcers in ferrets can be very dangerous if left untreated. Take your ferret to the vet if your ferret grinds his teeth (a sign of abdominal pain); has black tarry stools (a sign of blood in the stool) or soft, poorly digested stools; is lethargic; vomits or goes off his food. If your ferret has abdominal pain, he will likely eat less or stop eating, which will make him weak. Ulcers can lead to internal bleeding, which can cause anemia. If left untreated, the ulcer can cause hemorrhage and death.

Many stomach ulcers in ferrets are caused by a bacteria called *Helicobacter mustelae* (related to the bacteria associated with ulcers in humans). Your veterinarian will likely prescribe a bland diet and antibiotics and other medication to help get rid of the bacteria. Because stress can cause and worsen ulcers in ferrets, it is important not only to treat the ulcer but to remove the cause. Removing the cause(s) of your ferret's stress can help him to get over the ulcer. Avoid overcrowded cages, sudden or frequent changes in your ferret's environment and diet and keep a close eye on how your ferret reacts to additions of new ferrets or other pets to your household. If your ferret seems to be stressed by any given situation, try to avoid that situation, especially while your ferret is under treatment for an ulcer. Treatment of gastric ulcers may last up to two months in severe cases.

HAIRBALLS

Ferrets like to groom themselves and their friends. This can lead to hairball problems, especially in older ferrets. To prevent hairballs, give your ferret a half-inch ribbon of a cat hairball remedy (available at your local pet store or from your vet) three or four times a week during shedding seasons (ferrets change their coats in the spring and fall). Bathing and brushing are also recommended during your ferret's coat change. If your ferret is shedding and has a dry, hacking cough, he might have some hair caught in his throat. (However, a persistent cough could be a sign of a more serious condition and should be brought to the attention of your veterinarian.) You can increase the dose of cat hairball remedy to a half-inch ribbon once a day until the coughing stops. Your ferret will not cough up fur the way that cats do; therefore it's important to make sure the fur your ferret swallows moves through his gastrointestinal tract easily. Fur that is not passed through the gastrointestinal tract can accumulate in the stomach or intestines and lead to blockages. Blockages can become life-threatening very quickly, so hairball prevention should not be taken lightly.

HAIR LOSS ON TAIL

Perhaps the most common cause of hair loss on the tail is "rat-tail," a seasonal hair loss that may be a systemic reaction to stress. Ferrets can get acne on their tails, which can lead to hair loss. If your ferret has hair loss on his tail that coincides with a coat change and that starts at the tip of the tail and is accompanied by black dots on the skin, it is probably a case of acne (but see also "Adrenal Disease" above). Wash your ferret's tail using antibacterial soap or a mild benzoyl peroxide soap daily until the black dots disappear. The hair should grow back with the next coat change. If the hair loss spreads onto your ferret's back or does not seem to improve, see your veterinarian.

HEARTWORM

Depending on where you live, heartworm disease can be a serious concern. Because the vast majority of ferrets are kept indoors, heartworm is not a common problem in much of the United States. But if you live in an area where heartworm is prevalent—in particular, the southern United States—or if your ferret is regularly outside for long periods of time, heartworm is a very real concern. Fortunately, there is a way to prevent heartworm disease. Talk to your veterinarian about putting your ferret on medication to prevent heartworm. If your ferret is older than six months and has never been on heartworm preventive, you should have him tested for the presence of heartworms before starting him on the preventive medication.

HICCUPS AND COUGHING

For the most part, hiccups in ferrets are completely normal. When our Sabrina (the hiccup queen) gets a bad case of hiccups, water or a few licks of Ferretone usually gets rid of them. If your ferret is coughing, check to see that his throat is clear of any obstructions, like a piece of food or some other object he might try to eat. The best way to get a good clear look into your ferret's throat is to gently scruff him, which will make him yawn. Do not push the food or object further into his throat. If you can pull the object out safely, do so. If a piece of food is stuck, offer your ferret water, Ferretone or a cat laxative (like Petromalt) to help him move the object down his throat. Our Marshmallow is a fast eater and often ends up with a piece of food stuck in his throat, but he has always been able to dislodge the food on his own by coughing. If your ferret cannot breathe, take him to the vet immediately.

Heartworm is a real danger to the ferret who spends time outdoors. Talk to your veterinarian about preventive medication.

INFLUENZA

Ferrets can get the same flus that you and I can get. If you have a cold or flu, avoid handling your ferret. If you must handle him, wash your hands before you do and avoid breathing directly on him. Your ferret's symptoms will be similar to the symptoms you experience when you have a cold or flu: sneezing, runny nose and eyes (clear discharge), slightly decreased appetite, lethargy and sometimes diarrhea. Influenza in ferrets tends to last longer than it does in

people (up to three weeks). Although flus are usually
not life-threatening, they do cause discomfort and can
sometimes lead to more serious illness. If your ferret's
symptoms become worse, if he stops eating, the discharge from his nose becomes yellow or greenish or if
you suspect your ferret is having difficulty breathing,
don't hesitate to take him to the vet. Otherwise, make
sure he has plenty of water and lots of warm blankets.
Make sure he continues eating and drinking and let
him rest as much as he wants. And remember that you
can catch the flu from your ferret as readily as he can
catch it from you.

INSULINOMA (PANCREATIC TUMORS)

The symptoms of insulinoma are often not noticed
until the disease is quite progressed. The most common symptom, lethargy, can often be misinterpreted
as just getting older—especially because insulinoma
occurs in ferrets who are three to four years and older.
One of the major problems with insulinoma is that it
causes low blood sugar, which can lead to symptoms
such as lethargy, disorientation, drooling, vomiting or
pawing at the mouth, depression, rear-leg weakness or
loss of coordination and, in some cases, weight loss. In
severe cases your ferret might have seizures resulting
in jerky leg movements, vocalizations and involuntary
urination. Insulinoma can be treated with drugs or
with surgery. Many ferret owners choose to use both
methods of treatment. If your ferret has insulinoma,
you will need to discuss the best treatment for him with
your vet.

INTESTINAL BLOCKAGE

One of the most common causes of death in ferrets
is intestinal blockage. This should be reason enough
to fastidiously ferret-proof your home. A ferret's intestines are very narrow and can become blocked by
some of the odd things he decides to eat. Basically, ferrets can and will chew on and possibly swallow anything that is springy, spongy, soft or chewy. Some of the
more common items/substances that have been

removed from ferrets are: foam (e.g., earplugs, cushions, foam balls, shoe insoles), rubber (e.g., soft latex toys, rubber bands, balloons), cotton, string, sponges and hairballs (hairballs are discussed above). Ferrets can also become blocked by nuts, paper or plastic bags.

Signs of intestinal blockage include vomiting, refusal to eat or decreased appetite, dehydration, absence of stool, small or "skinny" stool, straining, lethargy and depression. If you notice any of these symptoms, take your ferret to the vet immediately. Your vet may be able to feel a foreign object inside your ferret, or he may want to x-ray or x-ray with barium. Keep in mind that foam will not show up on an x-ray and may be difficult for your vet to feel. Sometimes the blockage can be alleviated by giving laxatives; more often surgery is required to remove the object.

Partial blockages can be just as problematic. A partial blockage can be very difficult for your vet to diagnose because the symptoms are similar to those of other gastrointestinal troubles. With a partial blockage, your ferret may continue to eat some food and move his bowels, so it doesn't seem like a blockage at all. Unfortunately, many blockages and partial blockages are discovered only when an autopsy is performed to find out the cause of death. Your best defense is to keep a keen eye on your ferret whenever he's playing—especially when you first get him home. An intestinal blockage can kill a ferret within a couple of days. If you suspect your ferret has an intestinal blockage, get him to the vet—don't wait.

Ferrets will chew on anything from rubber bands to paper to sponges, which can easily block their tiny intestines if swallowed.

LYMPHOMA/LYMPHOSARCOMA

The most common malignancy in ferrets is lymphoma, or tumors of the lymph nodes. Sometimes it can be treated and put into remission with chemotherapy, but more often it is fatal within a few months. Basically, there are few symptoms to warn of this disease until it has progressed pretty far. Some of these symptoms you or your vet might see are enlarged lymph nodes, diarrhea, weight loss and weakness. One of the reasons it is recommended that ferrets four or five years and older have a complete blood workup is so that diseases like lymphosarcoma can be detected early.

There is also a form of lymphosarcoma that affects younger ferrets. In these cases, the ferret will usually have no symptoms until he has difficulty breathing. Often the ferret is misdiagnosed as having pneumonia or cardiomyopathy.

Know your ferret's normal activity level and behavior patterns so you will be able to detect possible symptoms early on.

PROLAPSED RECTUM

A ferret might get a prolapsed rectum as. a result of severe, chronic diarrhea or from descenting surgery. If you notice that your ferret's anus is protruding, red or swollen, you should have your vet check it out. Many times a soft-food diet and a nonirritating litter (such as pelletized newspaper litter) will give the ferret's anus a chance to heal. On occasion, however, ferrets need a couple of stitches to keep everything in place so that they can heal properly.

TUMORS (SKIN)

The vast majority of skin tumors on ferrets are benign. If you periodically check your ferret for odd lumps or bumps, you can catch skin tumors early, before they have a chance to spread or attach to anything below the skin. Your vet can remove the tumor and have it biopsied. Our Ralph had a skin tumor removed and he's fine. It was a minor procedure: He was in and out within a half-hour. Later in the day he was his usual self, playing with the other ferrets.

Urinary Tract Infection

Ferrets occasionally get infections of the urinary tract. If your ferret is drinking a lot of water or seems to be having difficulty urinating, or if the urine is unusually dark in color, take him to your vet. Urinary tract infections can be treated rather easily, but you do not want to delay treatment. These infections can progress up the urinary tract and potentially cause kidney infections.

Urine Drinking

Sometimes ferrets drink their own urine. Although it is a disturbing practice, it is nothing to worry about.

If your ferret's weight loss or gain is sudden and extreme, see your veterinarian.

Weight Loss or Gain

Ferrets' weight can vary greatly throughout the year. They tend to put on a good deal of weight in the winter and lose quite a lot again in the summer. Our boys go from three pounds at their heaviest to two and a half pounds at their lightest. Some ferrets vary more than this. If the weight loss is seasonal and coincides with a coat change, it is normal. If the weight loss or gain is sudden and your ferret's behavior has changed, see your veterinarian.

Enjoying

part three

Your

Ferret

chapter 8

Training and
Socializing
Your Ferret

Ferrets are very intelligent animals, and if you don't train them, they will train you. Ferrets can learn not only basic social skills, like using a litter box and playing gently with humans, but also some fun tricks like sitting up and rolling over. (To learn about tricks, see chapter 9.) Teaching your ferret good social skills is a must. An untrained ferret is like an untrained dog—unpleasant and potentially harmful. You would not let a puppy do as he pleases; don't allow your ferret to do so. Even though ferrets are small, they are fast and strong and can play very rough.

The key to teaching a ferret anything is consistency and patience. If you are not consistent in your treatment of your ferret, he will take it

as a sign to do as he pleases. This is especially important in teaching your ferret how to play with people.
Keep in mind that any training must be done in the
spirit of love. Ferrets respond exceptionally well when
they are treated kindly.

Nip Training

All baby animals nip. Young animals (even small children) tend to interact with their environment using
their mouths. Young animals also teethe. Everyone
knows puppies need to be taught that nipping is unac-
ceptable behavior. The same is true for ferrets.

*Ferrets play
roughly with each
other. It is your
responsibility to
show them the
proper way to
play with people.*

Keep in mind that, in most cases, ferrets nip far less
after reaching adulthood (at approximately six months
of age) than as kits. Also remember that when your ferret is teething, you will need to offer him an appropriate chew toy. Hard rubber dog toys work especially well
at this stage. Don't punish your ferret for trying to
teethe; he is, after all, only a baby.

During this time you can start to teach your ferret the
proper way to play with humans. We've had success
using Bitter Apple spray. When the kit is awake and in
the "play" mode, we spray the Bitter Apple on our
hands and play with him. When he nips at our hands,
he hates the taste and soon decides it's not fun to
nip the offensive-tasting human hands.

93

You might have a ferret that doesn't respond to Bitter Apple or Lime. Another useful tool in deterring nipping is scruffing. If your ferret grabs you with his teeth, immediately grab him by the scruff of the neck, look right into his eyes, and say sternly, "no" or "ouch." Unless you communicate with him, he won't know he's hurting you: The exact same nip on another ferret is considered play. When ferrets play with each other, they let each other know what acceptable limits are. It is the ferret owner's responsibility to "explain" to the ferret that the nipping hurts *and* that there are better ways of communicating and playing with people. Remember that your ferret isn't trying to hurt you; he is trying to play with you.

The key to nip training is consistency. You can't allow a nip sometimes and not others. It will only confuse your ferret. A method that I do *not* recommend is hitting your ferret on the nose. In most cases, you won't hurt him. Instead, he'll think you're playing (they can be tough animals!) and won't understand why you're angry. If you do hit him hard enough to let him know he has hurt you, you've probably hit him way too hard. Besides, hitting can make your ferret frightened of you and can actually make him bite more. A ferret who believes hands are things that hurt him will try to protect himself from any hand that comes near him. Instead, be patient with your ferret. He will learn.

Learning to Lick

Of course, teaching a ferret that hands taste bad can make him avoid hands altogether. After each session with the Bitter Apple, you need to teach your ferret that hands are friendly and nice to lick. We've used Ferretone (or any "lickable" treat) to help teach our ferrets that, although biting is bad, licking can be nice. After the kit has worn himself out a bit, we hold him and offer the treat in the palm of our hands (making sure to wash all the Bitter Apple off our hands first). He licks it and begins to learn that *licking* humans is nice (it tastes good). Eventually, your ferret will understand that biting is bad and licking is good. Tired ferrets are less likely to nip and less likely to struggle and squirm while being held. It is easier to create positive learning sessions by holding the ferret when he is already inclined toward better behavior.

Holding Your Ferret

Ferrets are energetic and playful, but you want to hold your little ball of fur. How do you get your ferret to relax in your arms? It is best to start with a sleepy ferret. Try to make the experience as pleasant as possible. Offer him a treat. If you get your ferret to associate treats and comfort with being held, he will want you to hold him. Be aware, however, that some ferrets like cuddling more than others, and males tend to be a little less rambunctious than females. Kits are so full of energy when they are awake that they are unlikely to tolerate being held at all. Be patient with your ferret. Let him run himself down before you try to hold him. As ferrets get older, they are more prone to being "lap ferrets."

Because ferrets love to play, "time out" can be an effective training method.

If your ferret nips you when you try to hold him, don't put him down. He will have you trained in no time: "Every time I nip you, you will put me down so I can play." Instead, gently scruff your ferret and say, "no." If you must put your ferret down, put him in his cage. Try not to reward bad behavior with play time.

"Time Out"

Because ferrets love to play, using a "time out" approach when they misbehave can be particularly effective. Some ferret owners keep a cat carrier handy for when a ferret plays too rough with them. This is especially useful if you have more than one ferret. The ferret in the carrier can see the other ferret playing nicely outside the carrier. When the ferret in the carrier calms down, he can come out again.

Training Your Ferret to Come

A ferret can have a very short attention span when he wants to. When he's in new surroundings, he is

Lap time with your ferret is easier after he has had plenty of exercise.

unlikely to respond to you. But sometimes new surroundings are dangerous and you need your ferret to respond immediately. It is always worthwhile to train your ferret to come to a specific type of sound like a special squeak toy, a bell or other loud sound that your ferret can hear from a distance. Make sure that every time you use this sound, and he comes, that you give him a favorite treat. He should have no doubt that he will be rewarded for coming to this sound. If your ferret is ever lost inside or outside your home, you can use the special squeak toy or bell to find him.

Walking on a Leash

If you choose to take your ferret for a walk, you will want to have your ferret on a harness and leash (see chapter 4 for information about leashes). Although some ferret owners have been able to get their ferrets to walk nicely on a leash, most of us are more likely to take our ferret for a drag than a walk. You will probably follow your ferret as he explores more than you will

have him heeling at your side. It is difficult to teach
him to stay nearby when there's a whole world of new
things to sniff. With a ferret, the function of a leash is
to keep him from wandering off, getting distracted
and forgetting to come back.

Litter Box Training

One of the great things about ferrets is that they can be
trained to use a litter box. Mothers will often teach
their kits to use a litter box if the kits are left with her
long enough. But because most ferrets are separated
from their mothers before this is done, you will have to
help your ferret figure it out. Ferrets naturally seek a
corner to use as a bathroom. When you see young ferrets in a cage, you'll notice that they usually use a corner of the cage as a bathroom. You can use this natural
behavior to your advantage in teaching your ferret to
use the litter box.

Your ferret's cage should be equipped with a litter box
of your choosing. Put only between a half-inch and an
inch of litter in the box. If you put too much litter in
the box it becomes a place for your ferret to play
instead of do his "business." Because ferrets don't
cover their waste like cats do, they really don't need
much litter on the bottom of the box. It is best, particularly during the training stage, to leave a bit of waste
in the litter box at all times so your ferret remembers
what the box is for.

Ferrets usually have to use the box within a few minutes of waking up. When you wake up your ferret for
play time, make sure he uses the box before you let
him out to play. It's also a good idea to let him get
some food and water before you take him out to play.
Ferrets can be clever, and many a ferret has faked
using the litter box in order to get out of the cage for
play time. Don't be fooled. (Marshmallow fooled me,
and boy did I feel silly.)

Once he has used the litter box, you can let him out
to play. Allow him only a small area to play in at first.
This will keep a small kit from being overwhelmed by

huge new things all at once. It will also help you to litter train him. Every half-hour or so during playtime,
place your ferret in the litter box in his cage. If he uses
it, praise him lavishly. If he doesn't, let him continue
playing. Any time you notice your ferret backing into a
corner, quickly move him into the litter box. Vigilance
is the key to training your ferret to use the litter box.
Once your ferret realizes what the litter box in the cage
is for, you and he are
ready to increase the
size of the play area.

*Show your ferret
to the closest lit-
ter box when he
starts to seek a
"bathroom"
corner.*

At this point, you
might want to add a
second litter box at
the far end of the play
area. Remember to
put some of his waste
in the new litter box.
If your ferret prefers a
particular corner with-
in his play area for his
bathroom, place the litter box in that corner. He is
more likely to use the litter box if he chooses where it
belongs. Again, watch your ferret as he plays, and if he
begins to back up into a corner, put him into the nearest litter box. If he goes into the litter box on his own,
give him lots of praise and attention. If you want, you
can give him a treat. The only problem with offering a
treat is that your ferret can fake using the box to get
the treat. You could end up being trained by your ferret in no time.

Continue increasing the size of his play area until he is
litter box trained in the entire area he will usually have
run of. If he experiences a setback, go through the
procedure again until he gets it right. Because a ferret's intestines are short, when he gets the urge to go
to the bathroom, it means *now*. If the litter box is too
far away, he will look for the nearest corner. For this
reason, you must have at least one litter box in each
room your ferret will be allowed to play in. Some large
rooms might need two litter boxes. Again, you might

want to let your ferret choose the corner(s) where his litter box will be. Many ferrets do well with going in the litter box, but most ferrets are never 100 percent reliable. Our Sabrina is 99 percent, but the rest of them tend to forget sometimes. I'm always thankful ferrets are small.

If you have a problem with your ferret consistently having accidents or not using the litter box in his cage, you do have some options. Ferrets generally will not eliminate where they eat or sleep. If your ferret uses an inappropriate corner, place a towel or blanket in the corner. Or you could put a small dish of food in the corner. One of these will usually deter him from using the corner as a bathroom. Thoroughly clean corners that you don't want the ferret going in to remove the smell. Don't use harsh chemicals. Also, be sure your ferret's litter box is not too dirty or too clean. Ferrets have been known to eliminate next to the litter box if it isn't clean enough for them. You should scoop out feces daily and thoroughly wash the box at least once a week.

A ferret is a joy to watch and to play with. Consistent, gentle and loving training will make your ferret well-liked by all. It will also make him happy, because his good behavior will bring him lots of love and attention—and, on occasion, treats.

chapter 9

Having
Fun
with Your **Ferret**

Ferrets are fun. That's why we keep them as pets. They remain as playful as kittens their whole lives. Entertaining your ferret can be entertaining for you too. You can play all sorts of games with your ferret, teach your ferret to do tricks and go places with your ferret.

Learning Tricks

Because he is very smart, your ferret can learn to do tricks. Ferret owners have taught their little friends to stay on their shoulder, roll over, sit up and many other types of tricks. The principles for teaching a ferret tricks are basically the same as those for teaching a dog: reward the desired behavior. Make sure the reward is something your ferret likes and that is not bad for him. For example, we usually use a drop or two of Ferretone as a reward. The key to teaching tricks is to use patience and many short training sessions.

Coming to His Name

Many ferret owners teach their ferrets to come to their names. Some ferrets learn not only their own names, but the names of other ferrets. One of the keys to teaching your ferret his name is consistency. Whenever you speak to your ferret, you need to use his name. Whenever you hold your ferret or give him treats, repeat his name over and over. Help him to associate the sound of his name with something pleasurable.

To get your ferret to come to you when you call him might take some time. You will want to start in a fairly small room or corner of a room. Say your ferret's name over and over and whenever he wanders over to you, give him a treat. Eventually, he will associate his name with coming to you to get a treat. Many ferrets will come running to the sound of a squeak toy. This can be used as the call signal or in conjunction with the call signal you want your ferret to learn.

Sit Up and Beg

Since ferrets tend to reach up to get to things they like, teaching them to sit up for treats is not very difficult. We even taught Ralph, who is deaf, to sit up in response to a hand signal. It's best to work with your ferret when he's calm or after he's had a chance to play a bit. Find a place where there are few distractions so he is more likely to pay attention to you. Use a treat that your ferret really likes but that doesn't take very long for him to eat. Try breaking up a treat into smaller pieces. This way you will be able to get him to do the trick several times in the space of five or ten minutes, before he gets distracted.

Start by crouching or kneeling far enough away from your ferret to prevent him from leaning on you when he reaches for the treat (about a foot). Then show the treat to your ferret so he knows what the reward is. You might want to let him sniff it in case his eyesight isn't very good. Hold the treat up over your ferret's head. If he tries to lean on you, gently push him back and try again. Whenever he successfully sits up without trying to climb on you to get to the treat, give him the treat. Go through this procedure in five- or ten-minute sessions over the course of several days.

You can also teach your ferret to sit up on command (whether or not you give him a treat). Every time you hold the treat above your ferret's head, say the word

"up" or any other word you want him to associate with doing the trick. It is best to use a one-word command. After several sessions, your ferret will begin to sit up whenever you say the word. If you have a ferret like Ralph who can't hear, you will have to use a simple hand signal instead of a word. We use an index finger moving in an upward

You can teach your ferret to sit up with a treat or hand signal, and plenty of patient training.

motion. At first, to get Ralph's attention, we'd hold the treat in the same hand we were using to make the motion. Eventually, he started to sit up in response to the finger motion alone. After only a few of these five-minute sessions, Ralph was begging for treats nearly all the time.

Roll Over

For this trick, you'll need to prepare in the same way as for sitting up: Let your ferret play a bit first, find a quiet spot with few distractions, and use a treat that your ferret likes and that he can eat quickly. Be aware that some ferrets don't like being rolled over and they will struggle against you. If your ferret seems distressed or upset, perhaps this isn't the trick for him. Our Ralph gets panicked if we try to roll him over, so we don't force him. Teaching your ferret to roll over is a little more complicated and may take longer than teaching him to sit up.

First, show your ferret the treat and say "roll over" while gently holding him by the shoulders. Roll him all the way over and give him the treat. Do this several times during a five-minute training session. Your ferret will probably be a little confused and might become distracted. Be patient. You will probably need to do this a few days in a row until your ferret becomes comfortable with you rolling him over. Once he allows you to roll him over easily, he's ready for the next step.

To teach "roll-over," show your ferret the treat and help him roll over until he understands what you want.

Everything is exactly the same as the first few days, except that you will be rolling over your ferret only three-quarters of the way, allowing him to do the last bit of the roll himself. Whenever he successfully completes the roll, give him the treat. Once he learns this, go to rolling him only halfway over, then only one-quarter. Finally, you should be able to simply nudge his shoulder to get him to roll over. Your ferret might grasp the entire concept at any point during the training, or he might require more time. Practice makes perfect with this trick. The more you work with your ferret, the better he will learn.

While you are teaching your ferret to roll over, you can use various commands to communicate with him: you can use a voice command, you can simply show him the treat or you might want to make a circle motion with your finger (especially if your ferret can't hear).

Other Tricks

Ferrets love to hide things, especially leather, shoes and dirty socks. Here's a fun trick you can show your friends that isn't really a trick at all. Make sure you try this on a friend who doesn't know that ferrets are crea-

Tug of war is a fun game you and your ferret can play together.

tures of habit when it comes to hiding things. Explain to your friend that your ferret is very smart and that he will put things where you tell him to. Most people will say, "of course he can," while thinking that you are just biased and maybe a little crazy. Then give your ferret something to hide, like a sock or a leather glove, and tell him to put it away. Watch your friend's amazement as your ferret stashes the item. To really impress your friends, choose an item your ferret usually puts in the same place (like a sock that always goes under the chair or a special toy that always goes behind the couch), and tell your ferret to put the item where he usually puts it. Your friends will think your ferret actually understands what you're saying. Try it.

Games to Play with Your Ferret

Ferrets love to play with other ferrets and with you. Over time, you and your ferret will make up games to play with each other. Some of the games ferret owners play with their pets are tug-of-war and tag. You could also hang a ball from a string attached to a stick (like a fishing pole) so your ferret can jump up and bat at it with his paws. Some ferrets particularly enjoy chasing and being chased by their owners. Any time you are playing with your ferret, keep in mind that he is small and loves to get under your feet. The more you play with your ferret, the more he will come to you when he wants to have fun. So get down on the floor with the little guys and enjoy yourself. Odds are your ferret will enjoy it too.

Fun Matches and Ferret Shows

Many local ferret clubs hold fun matches and ferret shows to help support their educational efforts and area shelters, to educatefellow ferret owners and to have fun. The shows usually take place March through June and September through November. Sometimes you can find a notice regarding ferret shows in local papers or at local pet stores. Many ferret shows are listed in *Modern Ferret* magazine or other publications.

At a ferret show, entries are judged on genetics, care and grooming.

Fun matches usually consist of entertaining contests like tube races, bag escapes or costume contests. These are usually designed as events to bring ferret owners together for socializing and fun. There are almost always vendors selling ferret-related items and things you can't find at your local pet store.

Often, more established ferret clubs hold ferret shows. These are similar in concept to cat and dog shows, but on a smaller scale. Ferrets compete for championship titles based on genetics and care/grooming. These are sometimes highly competitive shows, with ferrets from long lines of champions being entered by private breeders. There are several show sanctioning organizations, each with its own set of standards. If you decide you'd like to show your ferret, you should consider the various groups and their standards and choose the one that best suits your own beliefs. (See chapter 13 for the names and addresses of such organizations.)

Knuks was too tired after showing to enjoy the ribbon she'd won!

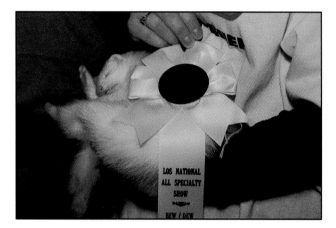

Ferret shows can be very exciting events. There are always vendors selling anything from basic cage supplies to unique craft items. Often private breeders will have kits for sale. Many clubs also include vaccination clinics at their shows. Ferret shows are also a great place to see all the different colored ferrets there are.

Short Trips Around Town

Since ferrets are small and can easily fit in a pocket, many people bring their ferrets with them on short trips around town. But if you will be going places where your ferret will not be welcome, leave him home. Don't create a situation where you have to leave your ferret in the car, especially during summer months.

When traveling by car, you should put your ferret in a pet carrier, even if it is only a short trip. Never let your ferret run loose in your car. Ferrets have gotten crushed beneath clutch and brake pedals, they've leaped out of sun roofs and gotten lost inside holes in the dashboard. Besides, what would happen if you had a car accident? A pet carrier is a wise investment that makes traveling safer and easier for you and your ferret.

Ferrets are relatively portable pets. Smaller "travel" cages can be equipped with all the comforts of ferret home and taken on the road. Many ferret owners adapt medium or large sized cat or dog carriers as ferret travel homes. A small litter box can be put in as well as food dishes and water bottle. A neat trick to create more space in a molded plastic carrier is to remove the top and fit a piece of fabric between the top and bot-

Your ferret will like to snuggle down in a pouch for short trips, but be sure not to take him anywhere he won't be welcome.

tom halves of the carrier, creating a second story/ hammock area. Secure the fabric with the screws that fasten the top to the bottom of the carrier. Alternatively, you could purchase a small wire cage for ferret travel.

Many ferret owners who travel by car on vacations bring their ferrets along with them. Remember that ferrets on vacation still need exercise. When giving your ferret playtime in a strange house or hotel room, make sure you ferret proof an area for him or keep him on a leash during play/exercise time. Always supervise your ferret's playtime when you are on the road.

Many hotels will allow your ferret to stay in the room with you as long as you keep him caged. Call ahead to check with any hotels or motels where you might be staying. If you are traveling to another state, it is a good idea to check that ferrets are legal in all areas you travel through. Some states require you to get a permit just to pass through with your ferrets. See chapter 11 for more about legal issues and traveling with your ferret.

Your ferret will give you years of joy and love. Playing with your ferret and involving him in your leisure time not only gives you an opportunity to be a little silly, but it also helps you and your ferret have a more solid and enjoyable relationship. The more time you spend playing with your ferret, the more he will enjoy spending time with you. And isn't that why you have a ferret in the first place?

chapter 10

Ferrets and Your
Family and
Friends

Many ferret owners are not only multiple-ferret owners, but also multiple-pet owners. Ultimately, how well your various pets will get along with one another depends on each one's personality. But your ferret will be interacting with people, too—other members of the family who live in the

house and any people who visit, like relatives or friends. Although every situation and every person and ferret is different, there are some guidelines you can follow to help maintain harmony among all the people and creatures in your home.

Ferrets and Other Pets

Anytime you introduce a new pet into your household, there is a potential for conflict with the animals already living there. You must

Ferrets tend to get along wonderfully with cats, especially if they were raised together.

supervise any meeting between two animals closely and carefully. Knowledge of the personalities of the pets already living in your home, as well as common sense, should guide you in bringing your pets together.

For the most part, ferrets do not mix well with rodents (gerbils, hamsters, mice, etc.) or birds. Other pets you should keep separated from your ferret are hedgehogs and sugargliders or any small animals that might be too delicate for ferret-type play. Snakes and other reptiles should also be kept away from your ferret. Some people may have no problem introducing their ferret to their iguana, but it is far safer to assume the two will not get along. While ferrets might show little interest in fish, it is best to keep the fish tank securely covered. You wouldn't want your ferret to fall in.

Most dogs and cats can become great friends with your ferret. Be sure to watch them closely the first few times they're introduced. Some dogs are not recommended with ferrets; terriers or dogs who have been trained to hunt small animals might consider your ferret to be dinner. Usually, cats and ferrets get along particularly well; this is especially

FERRET FRIENDS

Ferrets are sociable animals and tend to become great friends with dogs and cats.

. . . AND FERRET ENEMIES

Ferrets will naturally hunt rodents, so it's not a good idea to keep your ferret with guinea pigs, gerbils, hamsters or mice. Other small animals like chinchillas and rabbits might prove too tempting as well. Some breeds of dog, terriers in particular, were bred to hunt small animals (just about ferret size, in fact) and likewise should not be kept with ferrets.

true if they are raised together. Many people with both cats and ferrets claim that the ferret helps keep the cat playful through more of its life. Here, again, use common sense. If you have a cat who generally doesn't like any other animals, you might want to keep him separated from your ferret.

When you introduce your ferret to another pet in your family, make sure you are holding the ferret securely. Animals get enormous amounts of information through their sense of smell. Allow your two pets to sniff each other. If you notice any tension between the two animals, separate them and try again some other time. If the tension continues, you probably want to keep the two animals separated. If your pets seem to like each other, you can allow them to get acquainted

Ferrets and young children can be great friends, but play-time should be supervised.

while you are giving them your complete attention. Most cats and dogs are intrigued by ferrets and want only to figure out what they are. Be aware that large dogs might hurt your ferret without meaning to. Watching your pets when they play together can help avoid tragedies.

Ferrets and Children

No animal of any species should ever be left alone with a baby, small child or person of any age who is incapacitated. Contrary to some popular myths, ferrets do not eat babies or small children. They do not suffocate infants. They do not suck babies' blood. Most family pets are curious about the sounds coming from the bassinet, and ferrets are no exception—in fact, they're probably more curious. Use discretion when introducing any pets to your child. Not only could a pet injure

111

your child, but your child could injure your pet. Because ferrets should be kept caged when they are not out for supervised play, the chance of any injury to your child or the ferret is greatly minimized.

Some veterinarians and ferret organizations suggest postponing bringing home a ferret if you do not already have one and your child is less than three years of age. This is more to protect the ferret than the child. Although ferrets are relatively sturdy animals, if they are not held properly they can be seriously injured.

A ferret makes a fine pet in a home with older children. Ferrets are classroom pets in the upper grades of many elementary schools. Keep in mind that a ferret is not like a hamster; a ferret must be socialized like a puppy. If you want to get your child his first pet, but you don't feel he is ready for the responsibility of training and caring for a dog, he is probably not ready for

Teach your child how to treat your ferret well and hold him safely.

a ferret, either. How old a child should be before he is responsible enough to care for a ferret depends entirely on the individual child's maturity. Some twelve-year-olds are more capable of caring for a ferret properly than some fifteen-year-olds.

If you feel your children are mature enough to play with the ferret unsupervised, be sure they know who is allowed to handle the ferret and who is not. Some of their friends might also be mature enough— some might even have ferrets at home—but others might need to be supervised. As an adult, it is your responsibility to explain this to your children. If you have any doubt that your child's friends will properly handle your ferret, it is probably best to supervise them.

Ferrets and Strangers

If your ferret is meeting someone for the first time, he will be very curious. As a rule, ferrets are friendly and outgoing and will sniff the new person. Some people are frightened by a ferret's curious sniffing. Remember, even though you know your ferret is safe, others might not. A stranger's quick motion could frighten your ferret. You should also stay alert to jewelry your ferret might decide is a good toy. One of our ferrets chewed a friend's watch band. The same ferret has been known to try to steal bracelets and shiny necklaces right off the wearer. If the new person has handled ferrets before, this kind of behavior will likely not bother him. But if the new person has never held a ferret, he might be disturbed or even perceive the ferret's playfulness as aggression.

Introducing your ferret to different people and situations while he's young will help him become a better socialized and well-behaved pet.

The way to introduce a ferret to a stranger who has never met a ferret or who is nervous about touching a ferret is to hold your ferret under his front legs facing you and support his hindquarters with your other hand. This way you can offer the stranger your ferret's back to pet, and your ferret will not be able to sniff or grab at the person. This method is also ideal if your ferret has never been around anyone except you and your family, and you don't know how he will act toward strangers.

The vast majority of ferrets, when properly socialized, will not bite, though occasionally there is a ferret who is just not nice. Many times if a ferret bites it is due to lack of training by the owner. By introducing your ferret while he is young to the types of situations he will encounter, you will help him be more comfortable in these situations. Sometimes giving your ferret a

113

treat helps to calm him and make him view the new situation as a pleasurable experience. Introducing your ferret to the world in this manner is similar to introducing a dog to unfamiliar situations and people while he is a puppy.

Relatives, family friends or anyone else who might visit your home and handle your ferret should be given a brief lesson in how to hold him. We usually show our friends the proper way to hold a ferret, then we let them hold and pet the ferret for a few minutes. Unless we will be playing with the ferrets, we keep them in the cage during the rest of the visit. This cuts down on not only the possibility of someone mishandling the ferret, but also the risk of the ferret being stepped or sat on by a person who is not used to having ferrets afoot. If you're not sure whether your guests'

Introduce visitors to your ferret and give them a chance to hold him, but keep him caged while you are entertaining.

children will handle your ferret properly, it is probably a good idea to keep your ferret caged during the visit. You know how your children are with animals, but others' children might not have the experience. Keeping your ferret caged will reduce the risk of injuries to ferret or child.

As long as you use common sense, your ferret will be a welcome member of the family. Once your ferret is properly socialized and used to meeting new people in new places, he will be friendly toward just about everyone he meets. And he'll probably love all the attention.

chapter 11

Legal Issues
and **Ferrets** in Your
Community

Most areas of the United States have regulations or ordinances about all sorts of pets, and ferrets are no exception. The biggest confounding factor in regulating ferrets is that no one can seem to agree on how they should be classified. The United States Department of Agriculture (USDA) considers ferrets to be domesticated ani-mals, but some states have ferrets wrongly classified as wild animals. Still others consider ferrets to be exotic animals. How or whether an area regulates ferret ownership depends on how it classifies ferrets.

Regulations and laws regarding ferrets are always subject to change. Currently, ferret owners are actively working towards legalization, proper classification as domesticated animals (like dogs and cats) and creation of rabies quarantine periods. As of this writing, it is illegal to possess a ferret in California, Hawaii and the District of Columbia (Washington, DC). There are also a few cities and various counties where ownership of ferrets is prohibited. Some states require you to get a license in order to legally keep a pet ferret. The pet shop, breeder or shelter where you get your ferret should have information on the legal status of ferrets where you live and applications for any licenses you might need.

Victory in Massachusetts

Ferrets became legal to own in Massachusetts on March 7, 1996. The bill was passed unanimously and the governor gladly signed it. Many ferret organizations take this as a sign that ferrets are finally becoming better accepted as the enjoyable pets they are. Efforts to legalize ferrets in the various "ferret-free zones" are ongoing (see Chapter 13, "Ferret Resources," for organizations working on ferret legalization).

FERRET-FREE ZONES

Ferrets are currently illegal in California, Hawaii, and Washington DC among other places. Many other localities also prohibit ferrets as pets, but ferret advocates are working constantly to change these laws. (See Chapter 13, "Ferret Resources," for the addresses of organizations that are currently helping to legalize ferrets all across the United States.) If you are considering getting a ferret, or traveling with your ferret, make sure you know the laws of the area and act accordingly. In your community, contribute to ferret popularity by introducing your friendly ferret to neighbors and visitors and by being a responsible pet owner.

Know the Laws

Some places enforce their laws more strictly than others. For example, you cannot *possess* a ferret in California—even if you're just passing through. In New York City, however, enforcement is somewhat lax (the prohibition is actually a health department regulation, not a law, per se). If you are unsure of the laws in your area, contact a local ferret club or shelter, your veterinarian, pet shop or the state or local humane agency. Keep in mind that we have heard many stories of ferret owners being given the wrong information by state agencies and humane societies. Local ferret clubs are usually your best sources for current, correct information.

Because laws change and vary even from one county to the next, your best bet when traveling is to find a ferret group in the state(s) you're traveling through and ask them what the laws are and what you must do to comply. In some cases, you may have to obtain a temporary permit to travel through the state with your ferret. A list of groups and contacts is available from Shelters That Adopt and Rescue (S.T.A.R.*) Ferrets (see chapter 13 for the address).

Activists are working with legislators to get quarantine periods established in their states.

Rabies Concerns

Concern over rabies is very real in many parts of the United States. Although ferrets are indoor animals, they are still warm-blooded mammals and therefore can get rabies if they are bitten by an infected animal. Many localities require you to have your ferret vaccinated against rabies. It is highly recommended that you vaccinate your ferret for his own protection no matter what the requirements are where you live. For more about rabies vaccinations, see chapter 7.

For most domesticated species, local or state health departments establish quarantine periods for animals involved in bite incidents. Unfortunately, in areas where ferrets are illegal or misclassified as wild, there are usually no quarantine periods. Even in states where ferrets are classified as domesticated, there may be no quarantine period. This means that if your ferret bites someone and that person reports the bite to the department of health, your ferret can, and in most cases will, be destroyed and tested for rabies, even if he is vaccinated or has never been exposed to the virus. Kill-and-test policies are beginning to change in several states, most recently in New Hampshire, where there is now a quarantine period for ferrets involved in bite incidents. In any case, you will have a better chance of convincing a person not to report the incident if your ferret is vaccinated against rabies.

Help spread the word about what a wonderful pet your ferret is.

Shelters and Ferret Clubs

Most humane agencies and animals shelters do not deal with ferrets. In some cases, they have arrangements with local ferret shelters to pick up any ferrets that are turned in. In other cases, they simply destroy the ferrets, or an employee tries to find a home for them on his or her own. Depending on the legal status of ferrets in your area and the policies of your local animal shelter or humane agency, you might be able to locate a ferret shelter in your area by asking at your local animal shelter.

Ferret clubs are often part educational and part social organizations. Often they initiate or help support any ferret-related legislation in the area or state. They help to educate fellow ferret owners and the general public by putting on shows and having ferret education days at local pet shops. Most ferret clubs have members that are extremely knowledgeable about ferrets and can help both new and experienced ferret owners with any problems they might have.

Most humane society shelters don't accept ferrets, but ferret organizations across the United States have shelters to house and re-home ferrets.

How ferrets are perceived and accepted by our neighbors depends on how much we can help them understand about ferrets. Currently, ferrets are coming further out of the shadows as cherished companion animals. By training your ferret to be a good spokesperson (spokesferret?), you can help create the kind of image our pets deserve.

Beyond

the
Basics

chapter 12

Recommended Reading

Magazines

Modern Ferret. Crunchy Concepts Inc., P.O. Box 338, Massapequa Park, NY 11762.

Annual Publications

Ferrets USA. Fancy Publications Inc., 2401 Beverly Boulevard, Los Angeles, CA 92718.

Books

Bell, Judith A., DVM. *The Pet Ferret Owner's Manual.* Rochester, NY: Christopher Maggio Studio, Inc. and Miracle Workers, 1995.

Fox, J. G. *Biology and Diseases of the Ferret.* Philadelphia: Lea & Febiger, 1988.

Jeans, Deborah. *A Practical Guide to Ferret Care.* Miami: Ferrets Inc., 1994.

Morton. *Ferrets: A Complete Pet Owner's Manual.* Hauppauge, NY: Barron's Educational Series, 1985.

Winsted, Wendy. *Ferrets in Your Home.* Neptune City, NJ: TFH Publications, 1995.

Videos

Ferret Tales. hosted by Micki Wingate, President of the Great Lakes Ferret Association. Mosaic Video, (810) 777-2192.

Ferrets Unmasked. Beach Party Productions, 1223 Woodbourne Avenue, Baltimore, MD 21239.

13

Ferret
Resources

National organizations will not only provide information regarding ferrets but can also refer you to a club or shelter in your area. Write to each of these organizations to find out which one is right for you.

National Ferret Organizations

American Ferret Association (AFA)
P.O. Box 3986
Frederick, MD 21705

Ferret Fanciers Club (FFC)
713 Chautauga Ct.
Pittsburgh, PA 15214

League of Independent Ferret Enthusiasts (LIFE)
9330 Old Burke Lake Rd.
Burke, VA 22015

Legion of Superferrets (LOS)
P.O. Box 866
Levittown, PA 19058

North American Ferret Association (NAFA)
P.O. Box 1963
Dale City, VA 22193

S.T.A.R.* Ferrets (Shelters That Adopt and
Rescue Ferrets)
P.O. Box 1714
Springfield, VA 22151

United Ferret Organization (UFO)
P.O. Box 606
Assonet, MA 02702

Ferret Legalization Organizations in California

As of this writing, ferrets are illegal in California. These are the two groups working to change the law.

California Domestic Ferret Association (CDFA)
P.O. Box 1868
Healdsburg, CA 95448

Ferrets Anonymous (FA)
P.O. Box 3395
San Diego, CA 92163

Ferrets on the Internet

Many services such as America On-Line, CompuServe and GEnie have areas devoted to ferrets within their pet sections. Below are some of the other resources available on the Internet.

The Ferret Mailing List (FML)—To subscribe to the FML, send e-mail asking to be added to: <ferret-request@cunyvm.cuny.edu>

The Ferret Frequently Asked Questions (FAQ)— To receive a copy of the Ferret FAQ (©Pamela Greene), send e-mail to: <listserv@cunyvm.cuny.edu> with the following message: SEND ANSWERS PACK-AGE FERRET.

Ferret Central (with links to many other ferret-related websites) <http://www.optics.rochester.edu:8080/users/pgreene/central.html>

Usenet Groups: rec.pets, alt.pets.ferrets

Modern Ferret on the Web — <http://www.modernferret.com>

Other Resources

The National Animal Poison Control Center (a non-profit organization)—around-the-clock service by veterinarians. They will make follow-up calls as needed. Call (900) 680-0000. Charges are $20 for the first five minutes, plus $2.95 for each additional minute. Or, call (800) 548-2423, which charges $30 per case, payable by credit card only.

DATE DUE

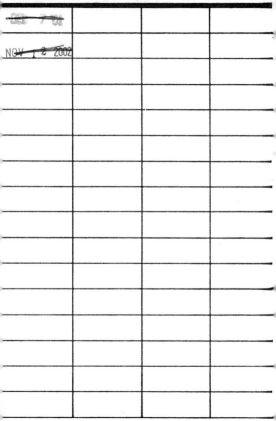

OCT 7 01			
NOV 1 2 2002			

#47-0108 Peel Off Pressure Sensitive